JOURNEY IN FAITH

REVISED EDITION

JOURNEY IN FAITH

An Inquirer's Program

Barbara Wolf

The Seabury Press / New York

1982
The Seabury Press
815 Second Avenue
New York, N.Y. 10017

Copyright © 1960, 1965; text revision copyright © 1982 by The Seabury Press.

All rights reserved. No part of this book may be reproduced, stored in a retrieval system, or transmitted, in any form or by any means, electronic, mechanical, photocopying, recording, or otherwise, without the written permission of The Seabury Press.

Printed in the United States of America

Acknowledgements:

The quotation from "Little Gidding" is from *Four Quartets* by T.S. Eliot, copyright © 1943 by T.S. Eliot; renewed 1971 by Esme Valerie Eliot. Reprinted by permission of Harcourt Brace Jovanovich, Inc.

Quotations from the Bible are from the *Revised Standard Version of the Bible,* copyright © 1946, 1952 by the Division of Christian Education, National Council of Churches.

ISBN: 0-8164-2402-0

Contents

ONE / Humanity   1
TWO / Sin   17
THREE / Redemption   34
FOUR / Church   49
FIVE / Sacraments   64
SIX / Prayer   80
SEVEN / God   94
EIGHT / The Last Things   106
NINE / Christian Personality   118

JOURNEY IN FAITH

ONE

Humanity

Journeys have one thing in common: they always start out from where we are. As individual travelers, we have quite different places to go, different routes, and different reasons for going. We choose to travel by bus or by plane, by car or by boat. A few of us have a lot of money to spend; more of us probably have to budget carefully. Some people look forward to sightseeing, others to meeting new people. Yet all of us start from our own front doors.

So it is with journeys in faith. We all start where we are, however different our ideas about our destination. Some of us do a lot of wandering about; some of us really know little about why we're going. Some of us are carrying a lot with us, but most of us have no idea what we need to take along. In reality, we start with no more luggage than our selves. We start with who we are.

Well, who are we? The question sounds simple enough, because we are all human beings. Yet, paradoxically, we find it difficult to say exactly what that term means. There are dictionary definitions of "human being," of course ("bipedal primate mammal"), but these are scarcely satisfactory. We can ask the experts and get a variety of opinions, but the professional people seem to be limited by their own concerns. To the doctor, we are physical organisms subject to injury and disease. To the teacher, we are heirs to an enormous accumulation of knowledge. The biologist sees us as the result of a long development of life on earth, while the chemist sees us as a combination of elements put together in a wonderful way. Anthropologists and sociologists see us as members of cultures and sub-cultures, while economists treat us as producers and consumers.

Who do we ourselves think we are? If asked point-blank, we are not likely to say we are composites of groups of interacting cells given shape by genes containing DNA. We are more likely to say, "I am So-and-So and I live in Such-ville." It hardly seems necessary for us to define ourselves as human beings—this is assumed before the conversation starts. There is an unspoken agreement among us all that we need not restate the obvious fact of our humanity whenever we meet one another.

It is when we are asked to describe ourselves in terms of our human-ness that the trouble begins. Intelligence? A person with an IQ of 50 is human, although elephants are smarter. Ability to communicate? Dolphins talk to each other. Loyalty? Love? Compassion? In some ways, our pets seem to behave more humanely than most people we know. Yet common sense as well as scientists remind us that cats and dogs are not human beings, but we are. Apart from our genes, what is it, then, that sets us apart from the rest of the animal kingdom? What makes us *human*?

One of the principal distinctions of human beings—and not a happy one—is that we struggle with problems that are more complex than those of any other animal. We have needs that extend far beyond the simple drives to survive and to reproduce our species. These problems and needs are recognizable in all of us, and they provide the motivation for much of what we do. Indeed, they form the basis of our understanding of each other.

Before we even begin to talk about God and religion, about the direction a journey in faith will take, we are going to have to know what our problems and needs are, because these determine our starting place. Like all travelers, we can't begin until we know why we wish to go. Knowing all that there is to know about God—whom we assume to be one side of any religious relationship—is like knowing all about the destination of a journey. If we knew, we would find we need never leave home.

It is a little difficult to describe a human being without giving some attention to the fact that he or she has two legs, two arms, a body, and a brain. We share with all animals the need for food and oxygen, and we share with all mammals the capacity to suffer from heat and cold, rain and snow, hunger and thirst.

This much is obvious. It does not distinguish us from other creatures. What is not always so obvious is that our physical bodies are essential to our personalities, to whatever it is that makes us human. Our bodies are tools, by which we shape our lives. For one thing, they provide us with the means to communicate with each other. While some of us are fond of talking about the importance of the "spiritual" or the "emotional," we need bodies to express that which we sense to be non-physical. We can and do produce thoughts, ideals, emotions, aspirations; but we do so with brain cells, and we communicate our thoughts with voices and hands, with bodies.

For better or worse, our physical characteristics also limit us, as a playpen confines a toddler. We cannot be in two places at the same time. Much as we would like to, we cannot all win Olympic gold medals, all play in the Super Bowl, all win the Boston Marathon—or, more to the point—all eat whatever we feel like eating. Our bodies are wonderful and complex machines, but they often turn out to be unreliable or unsatisfactory, and they have far more influence on the "spiritual" or "emotional" side of us than we realize. And inevitably when they stop working, we die.

Coming to terms with our physical needs and limitations is, for millions of people, a full-time occupation. In a famine, for instance, nobody has much time or energy to fret about the cost-of-living index. For that matter, the parent whose family must eat on a poverty budget is not inclined to be anxious about the children's Scholastic Aptitude Tests. Even for those of us who are neither starving nor poverty-stricken, our bodies can create unexpected, even cruel, problems. Mr. J. has a heart attack, for instance. He has to stop smoking and drinking, lose twenty pounds, and cut out the twelve-hour work day. He will, of course, try to follow the doctors' orders. He will also find that his image of himself has been rudely altered. He's no longer the person he once was. Mrs. S., too, must learn to cope with a traitorous body. She has arthritis. She cannot do the things she has always done. The constant pain is changing her from a loving mother into a depressed, whining, self-pitying burden on her family. Her body has turned out to be an unfaithful servant. That fact now governs her life.

Thus, we can say a little more about ourselves than that we are two-legged, two-armed animals who resemble the great apes. We work with ideals and hopes and ideas that we fondly assume to be the marks of our humanity. But—these hopes and ideas depend for their fulfillment on our physical ability to carry them out. If our basic physical needs are not met, we die. But if our physical limitations are too oppressive, we might just as well be dead. These facts are part of what we are.

"Freedom" has become a political catchword, its meaning almost lost in the contemporary shuffle of slogans and labels. We associate freedom with such things as the right to vote, the right to privacy, the right to own property, the right to free speech. If we get beyond the Bill of Rights, we might also assert cheerfully that a human being is an animal with freedom of choice—or who *ought* to have such choice.

Political freedom is not essential to our humanity. If it were, we would have to write off as sub-human the millions upon millions of men and women who have never known political or economic freedom, both our contemporaries and those who lived in past centuries. This we can scarcely do. People who live behind the Iron Curtain are still people. Slaves in every period of history are human first, slaves second.

The human cry for freedom comes from a deeper source. We want to be able to decide for ourselves, to make up our own minds, to make our own mistakes. If we cannot be free politically, we have to be free to think, to love, to laugh. Examples of the thwarted urge for freedom are all too common and all too tragic. A hard-line Communist party member, for instance, may be unable to decide about anything important until he gets the word from the Politburo, and may even be unable to read what he might otherwise like to read. To some of us, he may seem less the human simply because he chooses not to choose for himself. But we inhabitants of a "free" society have to look also at the psychological horror of the overprotective parent, whose little Billy is still "too young" at thirty to make his own mistakes. And we have to examine our own reluctance to think for ourselves.

Freedom of choice is, of course, greatly hampered by many circumstances, including our physical characteristics. Many of us have habits we would like to be rid of, simply because they limit our choices; but the habits prove stronger than our need to be free. Many of us cannot easily stop smoking. Many of us cannot always, for our stomach's sake, choose freely between a chocolate eclair and a piece of unbuttered toast. Then there are financial circumstances. Some of us cannot freely choose between a vacation in the Bahamas and a picnic in the back yard. Few of us can choose a Rolls Royce for the family car.

Our individual freedom to choose is greatly narrowed by law, as well as by social custom and convention. Has my husband been unreasonable about my job hours? I am not really free to poison his breakfast coffee. Murder is against the law. Do I feel like quitting my job and taking off for Tahiti? The painter Gauguin got away with it, but I have obligations here at home and I dare not be so unconventional. Do I yearn for a diamond ring in the jeweler's window? The law says I do not have the freedom to break the window and grab the ring.

The urge to choose for ourselves can (and frequently does) drive us to rebellion, not only against customs and conventions, but also against the law, even against those who are closest to us. Sometimes we simply ignore the things that limit us. If I want the diamond ring more than I believe in the law, I will take it, operating on the assumption that my freedom to have the ring is of greater significance than the possibility of getting caught and punished. Like Iron Curtain defectors, sometimes we succeed in forcing our way out of the circumstances that bind us: we leave home, quit a dreary job, revise our life styles. More often, we seek out and find small areas of life in which we can be our own masters: "This year I'm going to start a vegetable garden."

But many of us never quite succeed in rebelling; instead, we day dream. We tell off the boss—while we're shaving in the morning. We fantasize about fame and fortune. We picture ourselves as we will be "someday," when they've found a cure for whatever cripples us. In the meantime, we live in terms of necessity. What else is there for us to do?

As we know, to our personal sorrow, freedom of choice is not an unmixed blessing. Once we have it, we find that we aren't sure that we like it. For one thing, freedom carries with it those burdens we call "responsibilities." The unwed teenager, for instance, finding herself pregnant, may bravely claim her freedom to keep and raise her baby, only to be overwhelmed by the unexpected and unprepared for strains of motherhood. If we choose to live alone, we have to pay the rent by ourselves.

Because the effects of free choice so often turn out to be painful, it frequently seems that life was a bit easier back in the comfortable days of childhood, when people made all the decisions for us. The hurts and struggles of adolescence derive in large part from this problem of freedom. Adolescents spend several years, an incredible amount of energy, and enormous quantities of emotion in winning the freedom to decide for themselves. Yet they are dependent on their peers in ways which bewilder their elders. At the same time that they are insisting on being free to stay out late, they are following their crowd into the dangerous, if popular, territories of alcohol, drugs, and indiscriminate sex.

Teenagers can teach all of us something about our humanity: we really cannot bear to be alone. Like the ant, we are social beings, who cannot exist independently of our fellow creatures. The ant lives in a highly structured society, because he would not otherwise be able to eat. We need each other, not just to provide for our physical essentials, such as food and shelter, but because we want to *belong*. All of us, from the tiniest baby to the elderly stroke victim in a nursing home, crave the loving concern of other human beings. It isn't enough, for example, merely to feed and clothe a newborn baby; nor is it enough merely to take "adequate" physical care of the aged. Without the love of others, the human organism withers away and dies.

It is not difficult to measure the degree to which we are bothered by the problem of belonging. How comfortable are we, when we find ourselves alone? Are we content with the solitary decisions we make, or must we always seek the judgment and approval of others? If I do decide to run off with someone else's husband or wife, can I live with the hostility of my family? If I decide not to smoke pot, can I live with the derisive laughter of my friends? Some of us are so anxious to belong that we find ourselves physically worn out, trying to keep up with everyone around us. Some of us may spend most of our waking hours talking to our friends on the phone, so pressing is our craving to be heard and loved.

Yet our groups of friends are burdens, too. How can we be really certain that people love us? How can we be sure that we really belong? Just when we think we are warm and secure, things happen: someone new joins the group and gets all the attention; the old school bunch—the same people who represented our youthful ideals—drifts apart as the years go by; people move away; people die. We must continually juggle the problem of belonging, because there is no way we can make other people remain where we would like them to be, in a constant, supportive relationship with us.

Not only are we troubled by the difficulties and pressures involved in belonging, but at the same time we are painfully aware that we need to be recognized as individuals. We need space to express our uniqueness, as if for every moment we want to be doing things with others, we want to have some solitude, some time alone to be doing what we want to do. Each of us has his or her own special abilities, talents, dreams, even weaknesses. These, we feel, should (in a world that is fair and just) be counted.

Yet we find our problems colliding with each other. On the one hand, we clearly need to belong; on the other hand, we clearly need to be ourselves. The same friends on whom we depend for affection and acceptance also demand, in all sorts of ways, that we give up something of ourselves in order to gain that acceptance. Perhaps we have to be witty or wealthy or interesting in order to fit in. We may have to be fond of gossip or gardening or a certain political party before others will make us part of their crowd. We may have to experiment with drugs or sex to get invited to parties. We may have to bend our personal standards like so many pretzels in order to maintain our connections with whatever small worlds we find ourselves living in. Even our families—surely one kind of group that ought to be safe for individuals—frequently treat us as if we were more valuable for what we do than for what we are, especially as they persist in treating us as things, as breadwinners, unpaid household help, "kids," or "parents."

The human thirst for individuality is shabbily treated these days, but then it always has been. Non-conformists have never been popular. Even when non-conformists manage to make names for themselves, they become models for those who turn what was once a rebellion of individuals into new forms of groups, rules, regulations, and all. Those who would imitate Thoreau and live alone in the woods attract followers and produce communes. Furthermore, the rules that hold groups together, that give us directions for belonging, keep changing. Years ago, in some places, we had to drive big station wagons if we wished to "belong". Now the same vehicles make us look like greedy egotists.

The man or woman who dares to express individuality is running a serious risk. We may secretly envy such daring, but for the most part we have enough nerve to assert ourselves only so far and no farther. To some degree we are always stopped by our fear of "what people will say," by our parallel need to be loved and accepted by others.

Along with our need to be accepted and loved by others, and our need to be valued as who we are when we are alone, we want to love. That is, we want to cherish and care for other people, to do things for those we love, to make other people happy, to give presents, to help.

Nothing is so disheartening as the feeling that we are not needed, and it frequently appears that we aren't. It is instructive, if painful, to reflect seriously on how much we really matter in the lives of those around us. *Are* we needed?

A lot of people seem indifferent to our love. They don't like the presents we give them. They resent being cherished. Even our own children ignore with distressing regularity our deep feelings toward them, apparently convinced that our love and concern for them is part of some dark conspiracy to deny them their freedom.

When there is no one around who wants our love or who needs us, we are forced to lavish our attention on something else—on pets, much of the time, or on hobbies, or on causes. There is no question that these are meager substitutes for people; but for many of us there is no other outlet for our need to care for someone besides ourselves. Those of us who have not yet been touched by the pain of this human need shake our heads in disbelief at newspaper items about elderly ladies who keep twelve cats or about wills directing that large estates be left to faithful dogs. We might reflect on the power of the human need to give love. We may deplore the fact that some parents endure, without complaint, humiliating treatment from their young, and yet we all appear willing to undergo painful circumstances, as long as we are allowed to go on loving those who matter to us. The nagging loneliness that so often attacks us in the middle of the night comes not only from the conviction that no one loves us; it can rise also from the perception that no one needs us.

Only a very select few human beings do things that change the world. Most of us see ourselves as doing our small jobs, going to work, changing the diapers, trying to stay within the budget, having a little fun now and then—but for all that we do, we accomplish relatively little of significance. There has been only one Shakespeare, one da Vinci, one Beethoven. For that matter, there has been only one Julius Caesar and one Albert Schweitzer.

Despite this, we all seem to need to produce or create something that will outlast our very ordinary daily existences. We watch the absorbed delight of a small child at work with crayons or fingerpaint and notice the power of our human creative urge. If we are honest with ourselves, we do tend to envy the children. For them, the happiness is in the doing, not in the finished product—in the praise of adults around them, not in the monetary value of the pictures.

For us, it isn't so easy. We rarely get the chance to feel that what we accomplish is useful or good or beautiful—or even appreciated. Sometimes we do manage to create something that pleases at least ourselves; but we certainly don't get appreciated in the coin of the realm.

Our need to be creative is rarely recognized for what it is. Rather, we find ourselves complaining that our jobs are boring, our daily routines are dull, our lives are "unfulfilled," our existences unimportant. Hobbies become something to fill up spare time. Most of us let television do our creating for us.

Our technological civilization makes the problem worse. Automation has tended to remove whatever satisfaction men and women once had in their work; frozen dinners take away the adventure of cooking. Indeed, very few of us ever see the finished product on which we are working. Surveys that show increasing dissatisfaction with the quality of our jobs are saying more than we perhaps have noticed. We may say we want more leisure, when actually we have nothing to do in our leisure time. If we are fortunate, we find time to make or do *something*, but for most of us there is not enough time or energy to quiet our restlessness, primarily because we don't know where it comes from. So we hit our thumb with the hammer and go back to the routine at the plant, with one more need unsatisfied. Tomorrow we'll build a barbecue in the back yard or join a volunteer group; but tomorrow never comes for many of us.

Ever since human beings, wandering around in a large and terrifying world, became conscious of their vulnerability, they have demonstrated a universal need to worship. That is, wherever the human race has found itself, it has found the universe an awesome place, unpredictable, dangerous, and powerful.

Hence the human tendency to attach importance to something or someone stronger, for protection, perhaps, or at least for direction. Human beings look for meaning in an existence that more often than not seems formless and chaotic. And whenever they find the prospect of protection, direction, and meaning, they pay special attention. They acknowledge the superior worth, the worth-ship, of whatever embodies that prospect.

Deep within all of us is the awareness that we are not self-sufficient, either as individuals or as a species. We depend on forces we cannot control. We did not come into the world by our own choice or power, and we have very little to say about the way the world runs, whether we are talking about natural laws or about political systems. To be sure, we can look at the accomplishments of our race, credit ourselves with having "conquered" space, having split the atom, and having eradicated small pox. Yet we still are at the mercy of floods, earthquakes, storms, crop failures, famines, and so on. We still all die.

The natural forces of our universe operate without reference to our achievements. The only way in which we can get along is by paying strict attention to such non-human factors as the laws of physics. We cannot change those factors; all we can do is live with them. Since we are not really masters of our own fates, we have the deep-rooted suspicion that we had better pay attention to whatever or whoever is in charge.

Furthermore, because we live with other human beings in communities, we find ourselves having to pay attention to the people who have power over us. Here again, we are not free to control our own lives. Whatever our status, there always seems to be someone with more power than we. Consequently, even those of us who rarely contemplate the unpredictability of Mother Nature feel keenly that we can't fight City Hall, that we cannot shape the decisions which directly affect us—the price of heating oil, the mortgage rate, or air pollution. We feel that we only obey the law, that we have little to say about what the law *is*, despite the fact that we live in a republic.

It is our need for protection and security, for a sense of direction and stability, that emerges in the human activity called worship. Everyone worships, even agnostics and atheists, because everyone acknowledges the "worth-ship" of some person, some ideal, or some belief, of something that gives meaning to life. Our objects of worship—our gods—don't have to be natural forces, like the sun or the sky. They don't have to be heroic figures from myths. They don't have to be scientific dogmas. We certainly don't have to worship the Judaeo-Christian God. Our gods can be our families, our husbands or wives or lovers, our businesses, our country, even our Bibles and our "religions." Whatever will best serve to keep us from falling into the abyss of meaninglessness and despair, that is what we worship.

Our personal attempts to attach ourselves to our gods sometimes seem curious to other people. Furthermore, these attempts usually prove to be inadequate. They are often inexplicable to those around us who are worshiping something else. For instance, many of us give our hearts to "causes" ranging in size from service clubs to national politics, from zoning regulations to constitutional amendments. Since other people have given their hearts elsewhere, we can't even talk to them about our beliefs. Frequently these causes have very little to do with our private lives, which is one of the reasons that our private lives seem so aimless.

Naturally, we prefer to attach ourselves to causes and heroes of some clear merit, to things of generally recognized virtue. But there have been times when our causes were morally indefensible and our heroes grotesque. Millions of Germans followed and worshiped Hitler with great willingness. Few in contemporary society would adopt Hitler as a god, as few Americans would acknowledge Lenin as worth worshiping. But there are many grotesque gods around, and they have a lot of followers. The fact that we deplore tragedies like the mass suicides in Guyana does not mean that we are more justified in *our* causes. We are only choosing to worship in ways generally regarded as more respectable, more acceptable.

What if we recognize the futility of causes and heroes? What if we decide that it isn't getting us anywhere to worship the gods of family and business? Do we go back to the God of our childhood? Some of us try. We read the Bible, perhaps, and we notice that, to this day, we see God as an elderly gentleman in a long white beard, who is mostly kind, but sometimes apparently deaf. What has this figure to do with the world we live in? With the starvation of children in Asia and Africa? With the slow agony of terminal cancer? With the tornado that demolishes a hospital? What does this kind of god have to attract and hold our attention?

If we were to make a list of human needs and ask our friends what they thought to be the most compelling, chances are most of them would say something like "peace." By this they do not necessarily mean peace among nations, although in a world so precariously unstable as ours, that kind of peace takes on increasing importance. They may also be talking about "peace of mind." The shocks of contemporary life—crime, unemployment, inflation—enhance our sense of the fragility of our security. The regularity with which our lives are unsettled and our apple carts overturned makes us yearn for stability. We need to feel that death and taxes, to say nothing of pain, poverty, and war, are not the only certainties in human existence. Somehow, unless we are among the very select few who have managed to come to grips with life as it is, even in our happy moments we feel the urge to knock on wood. In the back of our minds echoes the eternal question "What if something happens?"

And, because we find our internal battles so costly, we realize that stability within a wildly changing external world is not enough. We need some peace within ourselves, perhaps even more urgently than we need peace around us. We look for, and fail to find, ways in which to balance the conflicting demands of freedom and love: the rise and fall in the popularity of alternatives to marriage provide an example. We may be harboring an acute sense of self-loathing, because we failed someone who needed us. We may discover, to our horror, that we actually hate someone we thought we loved. We try to do the right thing and find that we do the opposite of right, or that we can't figure out what is right and what is wrong.

The craving for peace is one craving which is rarely filled. Even when things go along smoothly and we are pleased with ourselves, we are nagged by the conviction, born of bitter experience, that interior peace doesn't last long. To make the problem more painful, we know that once we have misplaced peace, we have a hard time finding it again. Harmony and good will cannot be ordered when they run out, as if they were commodities on the market. They seem to come and go quite independently of us.

But we try. Although it proves to be painful and unproductive, the pursuit of happiness is enshrined as a sacred right, and we continue to pursue. Some of us try to make enough money, in the debatable assumption that economic security equals peace. Some of us retreat from the world into dreamlands of our own devising, into drugs, alcohol, and odd cults. Most of us wait for a golden opportunity, always hoping that someday our prince will come.

In our daily lives—and all lives *are* daily—whatever peace we enjoy is based on compromises. We cannot cope with the sum of our needs, so we look here and there for temporary solutions. We shop around for a religion, we buy books on the joys of sex, on security in the coming Armaggedon, on pain-free dieting. We manipulate our friends and families so as to keep them close to us. We sample a bit of freedom here, a commitment there. But the fact of the matter is that we are not peaceful creatures. We are at odds with the world, with each other, and with ourselves.

The bitter truth is that, however hard we try, we are never able to solve all our problems or satisfy our own needs, because, although we see ourselves as divided up into characteristics, into bits and pieces of needs and wants like parts of a jig-saw puzzle, we really are organisms. Our human characteristics do not exist in separate departments. They interact. If we spend our energy satisfying one need, another is affected and demands attention. If we start talking about human beings as having bodies and souls, we may start trying to treat our bodies as separate from our selves. Then we wonder why some illnesses can't be treated with antibiotics. Furthermore, as long as we think of our needs and characteristics as pieces of a jig-saw puzzle, we will try to force them into a recognizable picture and find that what we get is a bunch of nonsense.

Why do we have to be this way? Why are we the way we are? It is obvious that we are not alone in our misery. All human literature, for instance, from the beginning of poetry to the contemporary novelist, records the same story we see in our own lives.

The real pain of being human rises from the fact that we cannot ultimately solve our existence to our own satisfaction. We really ought to be able to describe ourselves as living organisms who are creative, who love and are loved, who are free to choose, to worship, and are peaceful. Instead, we find ourselves admitting, if we are honest, that we are beings who cannot, like Humpty-Dumpty, put ourselves together once, let alone again and again.

If we are creatures with such a striking list of attributes and potentialities, what in the world is the matter with us? Why can't we come to terms with our human nature? Dogs and cats do not appear to object greatly to being dogs and cats. Why is the human being the only creature who seems incapable of enjoying his or her own nature?

And what do we expect from a journey in faith?

We usually want to know first of all what makes us the way we are. This is the point from which all journeys in faith begin, because this is the point where we acknowledge our need to get away from our situation into a new one. Hence, we usually begin by asking for explanations of our unhappy state of affairs. But more urgently, we want an answer or a solution. At the very least, we want hope for the future, something to look forward to, a destination in which we can be rid of our disorder.

All religions have their explanations of life, from the concept of jealous spirits to "negative thinking". Almost all religions give hope for the future: Mohammedans look forward to Paradise; ancient Greeks offered the Elysian fields; Buddhists anticipate nirvana. In every case, the hope is a deferred one. We are told that the world—and the human race—is a mess and that we are going to have to wait for death to release us to a happier state. Our job is to do the best we can, according to the rules of the game, to win ourselves a place in that happy ending.

Christianity is a little different. It also offers hope, but the hope it holds out is more than simply a deferred one. We will be exploring, in this journey, just what Christianity has to say about our problem and about the kinds of hope it offers.

TWO

Sin

It is a curious fact of life that from the moment we begin to examine the human situation we run away from what we find. If at all possible, we deny that our needs and problems are tangled in complex and conflicting ways, and that if we attend to one aspect of our humanity, some other aspect demands attention, in a never-ending succession of clashes. We like to trace our difficulties to manageable sources, and we persist in trying to find simplistic solutions. For instance, we tend to blame.

Usually we blame other people—parents, educators, employers, children, "the system," or whatever. We didn't get enough love when we were young; we didn't have the same chances in life that other people had; things aren't what they used to be. Of course, sometimes we indulge in self-blame. This tactic leads to the "if only" position: if only we were better people, if only we could be more attractive, if only we could express ourselves more clearly, then our lives would be full of peace.

The simple response of blaming does not normally prove helpful, so our search for solutions extends to a search for causes. Is the cause of human suffering to be found in our governments, our laws, our moral standards (the ones said to have declined so markedly)? Have we not educated our young sufficiently? Have we tinkered too much with our world? Whatever abstract conclusions we come to, the impulse seems always the same: find out what (or who) is responsible for the human dilemma, then remove or reform the cause and the problems will all go away. Very few people go so far as to write up programs for ideal worlds, as did Plato, St. Thomas More, and Karl Marx. But all of us have our secret visions of Utopian worlds, in which human beings like us are made happy according to our capabilities.

One common assumption is that only *this* generation, *this* group of people, or *this* person (me, that is) suffers internal pain. Sometimes we like to think that fifty or a hundred years ago, there lived a happier race of people, with stable family lives, simplicity of life style, hard work bringing proper rewards, respect for law, religion, and thrift. Quite apart from the fact that a hundred years ago things were *not* all that rosy (as we realize when we start thinking about poverty and hunger and smallpox), we would be hard put to insist that people were markedly different in the 1800s, or at any other period in recorded history. All generations have always faced the same problems we face. They have always asked the same questions and suffered the same pain. The only differences between us and our forebears are those of landscape and custom, just as the only difference between our individual selves and people we live with is circumstantial. Thus, the corporate executive, who, fed up with life in the competitive jungle of business, decides to go "back to the land," back to that vision of a simpler existence, finds that he has taken his humanity with him. All that he has changed are his surroundings. Indeed, we always take our humanity with us, wherever we go in search of peace.

For whatever reasons, some people seem not to feel much pain at being human. All of us know a few of these lucky souls. They are the people who never worry about their health, because they are healthy; who aren't trying to be free, because they don't feel constrained; who are loved and who love, or at least have no evidence to the contrary. They love their jobs, have interesting hobbies, sleep well at night, raise ideal children, and never worry about the future. Their lives are like the Christmas letters we get from distant friends, with not a single thorn in a garden of roses. Indeed, all of us know something about being lucky. We too have our moments of peace and security. Today may be one of those good times: we are able to feel good about ourselves and those around us.

The difficulty is that even for the lucky ones, as for those of us who feel good temporarily, there remains the bitter truth that the world we all must live in is characterized by estrangement, suffering, malice, hatred, and violence. Our friends' marriages disintegrate; our friends' children are arrested by police; our friends lose their jobs, get sick, have breakdowns. And on a broader scale, people starve, even in our own affluent culture. Refugees cling to life in indescribable squalor. Bystanders are killed in senseless riots. Wars are fought for obscure reasons over the bodies of those who had nothing to do with political struggles. There is no peace within the human race, even as we congratulate ourselves for having won temporary peace in our hearts. And, always, human beings die, no matter how lucky they are.

One effect of our having to live in such a world, with fellow creatures like ourselves, is that we find our happiness to be very fragile indeed. As long as there is no peace around us, our own peace is always in jeopardy. What John Donne wrote three hundred years ago summarizes what we perceive about ourselves:

> "No man is an island entire of itself. . . . Any man's death diminishes me, because I am involved in mankind, and therefore never send to know for whom the bell tolls; it tolls for thee."

We are inextricably linked together in our common sense of who we are. Most of us are to some extent acquainted with the Judaeo-Christian explanation for the unhappy state of the human race. We have picked up our information from many sources—Sunday School perhaps, jokes and cartoons, things that agnostics say, as well as things that the "born-again" say. One very common summary of the Judaeo-Christian explanation of our predicament runs something like this:

Once upon a time, a man named Adam and his wife Eve made a terrible but understandable mistake. They ate an apple God had told them not to touch. It was Eve's fault, because a snake tempted her, and she tempted Adam, poor fellow. Because they had disobeyed God, he got angry and told them to get out of the Garden of Eden. Ever since then, He has been punishing us for Adam's mistake and Eve's foolishness. We are (presumably) so bad that God won't have anything to do with us unless we make ourselves over into sour, fun-hating, puritanical fanatics.

If this has been our understanding of Christianity's explanation of the human pain that we must live with day by day, no wonder we find the story unsatisfactory. If one of our children is into drugs, what difference does that apple make? What have two people like Adam and Eve, who lived thousands of years ago (assuming we can believe that they ever did exist) have to do with our loneliness? And why should anyone wish to worship so capricious a God, a God who would make such a fuss about an apple?

It needs to be said, in the first place, that the book of Genesis, the Biblical source of the Adam and Eve story, never was intended to be factual history for either the creation of the universe or the two individual people named Adam and Eve. The controversy surrounding the teaching of evolution in public schools, for example, misses the point that the creation stories are not—never were—designed to be scientifically accurate. Science was not part of the intellectual framework within which the people who wrote the narratives lived and thought. The Bible was written in circumstances foreign to us. The book of Genesis is an expression, in dramatic form, of a very great insight into the roots of our existence. Using narrative language, it seeks to explain how we came to be as we are, why we are at odds with ourselves, and why our humanity is often such an intolerable burden.

The theme of the story is simple enough. God—as presented in Genesis, more as a supra-human being than as Being itself—created the Adam in a state of natural happiness. (Adam is not, incidentally, a man's name. It is the Hebrew word for "human being.") He made the Adam a physical being, much like the other creatures, but with some of the characteristics of His own personality—"in his own image." He made the Adam a free creature. He gave the Adam the ability to love and be loved. He endowed the Adam with an intimate relationship to Himself. Because all these characteristics worked together harmoniously in the Adam, he was at peace with himself and with God. The Garden of Eden represents this peace. It symbolizes the Utopia we all sense to be the right human state of being.

Then, at some point in humanity's earliest history—and it makes no difference how many thousands or millions of years ago, or whether one or more persons were involved, or who started the whole thing—human beings rebelled against God and against their dependence on Him. It could easily have been as trivial a rebellion as the eating of forbidden fruit, although in the story the fruit represents the knowledge of good and evil. Whatever happened, and whenever, they became conscious of their freedom, conscious of themselves as possessing the power of self-determination, conscious of their ability to choose between good and evil. In sum, they became *self* conscious.

For the Adam, as for all human beings, this rebellion turned out to be catastrophic. The uncomplicated happiness of Eden depended entirely on a harmonious relationship with God. Now that relationship was ended, and the world was different and frightening. What had been natural became strange and menacing. As we all do, the Adam found to his dismay that he could not be his own creator, simply because, although he perceived in himself many of God's attributes, he really was a limited, created, weak little thing. He could not take care of himself. He could not be "in charge".

The story goes on to show how, when the old relationship with God had been broken, the loving Creator became an object of fear: the Adam "hid from the Lord God among the trees of the garden." (Gen.3:8) The peace represented by the Garden of Eden was irrevocably shattered. This is Biblically described as exile: "So the Lord God drove him out of the garden of Eden; . . . He cast him out, and to the east of the garden of

Eden he stationed the cherubim and a sword whirling and flashing to guard the way to the tree of life." (Gen. 3:23–4) The Adam, and all human beings, were allowed to do things the human way, but the price has been paid (for the original human decision) by every generation.

The story in Genesis goes on to describe how the initial rebellion spread like a cancer to relationships among human beings. Cain kills his brother Abel, thereby demonstrating the murderous consequences. When human beings try to regain communication with each other, the tower of Babel results. As the early books of the Bible detail the doings of men and women, we see the problems of humanity multiplying much as they do in our own lives. Generation after generation has sought to find its way back to the simplicity of the garden. We have tried everything, from human sacrifice to laws to education to philosophical ideals, as means to regain an innocent relationship with God and each other, even though we rarely know that it is innocence we seek.

So here we are today, still grappling with the Adam predicament. Instead of *being* loving creatures, we are forced to search for love. We are not peaceful, we are not secure, we are not content with our consciousness of who we are. Because we have lost our relationship with the eternal God, we look everywhere, in the most unlikely places, for adequate gods in this world.

Rebellion of humanity against God, and against ourselves, is the cause of all our problems, just as it is the reason for our inability to solve our problems. Once we have become *self* conscious, we cannot be our innocent, unknowing selves. We have fallen out of our given order in the scheme of creation. This condition of dis-order is what we have learned to call *original sin*. It is our inborn, inherited, habitual condition of estrangement from God and from each other. We have separated ourselves from our true place in the universe, and we don't seem to be able to get back again. Nor can we live as we know we ought, in the place we have made for ourselves.

Is this too strong a description of our lives? We can all think of instances in which human beings have managed to live peacefully, creatively, and generously, apparently untrapped by the traps we are caught in. Yet when we check the life stories of these people, we find that they too have endured the same mental pain we undergo, even if they have managed it better. And in any event, what matters to us is not what others have done with their lives. It is not important to us that Albert Schweitzer or St. Francis of Assisi seemed to escape the burdens we carry, not when we can't even stick to a diet. What does matter to us is what we see in our own mirrors, our own families, our own world, and our own consciences.

As we thrash about, trying to work out the problems that plague us, we find our behavior inclining toward certain habitual patterns, most of which get us into trouble with the world around us, all of which make us feel worse about ourselves. These are the activities that bring down on our heads the disapproval of moralists and reformers. They are what we normally think of when we see the word "sin".

To distinguish between sin as a fundamental condition of human existence and the various "sins" we fall into as we try to cope with existence, Christian theology makes a distinction between original sin and *vices* or *transgressions*. The vices are what result from our efforts to dull our pain or to insure our own security or to take charge of ourselves. As we look at them, if not in others at least in ourselves, we discover them to be natural concerns which are not, in and of themselves, bad. In fact, they are linked with the abilities, aptitudes, and appetites we have already identified as making us human. The difficulties these characteristics get us into arise as we try to use what is natural either as solutions to our basic problem or as anesthetics to disguise what is really wrong. When we perversely use what is given as "good," the effect is "bad" behavior.

Very few of us have been conspicuously successful in dealing with our vices, for they grow from the root problem of original sin. As we try to do something about them, we find ourselves handicapped, not only by our unwillingness to recognize their source, but by our inability to do anything to heal the original sin that gives them their power. Vices are, in one sense, like symptoms of a disease. The symptoms themselves are destructive. Because they usually are obvious, they draw our attention away from the disease itself. In another sense, vices are methods of coping with pain, like fumbling, clumsy responses to disease. However we look at them, they are always signs of the deeper disorder. The vices traditionally have been grouped into seven categories:

Sloth is what happens to our need for rest and relaxation. All animals, including human beings, must have a certain amount of time off, for sleep, for quiet, for solitude, for recreation. If we indulge in rest as a way of coping with the pressures of life, however, we become what people call lazy. People who aren't afflicted by sloth are likely to assume that others are lazy, because it is more comfortable to sleep than to work. But laziness is much more than that.

Sloth takes many forms. When parents are constantly and loudly pushing children, telling them what to do, forcing them to conform, children respond rebelliously—by doing nothing. It's their way of declaring independence. Then again, some of us adults are reluctant to do more than the minimum demanded of us in our jobs: we grab our paychecks and run, using sick days to extend holiday weekends. Some of us are loath to use our minds; it is easy, and (on the whole) safe, to let other people do the thinking and tell us the answers, particularly when we are afraid of our own answers. Most of us are unwilling to deal with our problems. It somehow seems less painful (for the moment) to run away from a decision than to risk making a wrong one. And of course all of us find it relatively easy to see sloth in other people, relatively difficult to see it in ourselves. The wife who nags her "lazy" husband for not getting chores done may not be aware that she herself enjoys not using her mind. The husband of a woman who works outside the home may complain that his wife is too "lazy" to bake her own bread, while ignoring the fact that he watches Monday night football while she cleans the house. All of us exhibit sloth. We just show it in different modes.

Gluttony is unnecessary preoccupation with food and drink. The physical need for nourishment is distorted into excessive forms that have little to do with the body's demands, but have everything to do with our vague discontents. The comfort of being fed is something to which we are legitimately entitled, by virtue of our humanity. The preoccupation with food and drink that afflicts the starving is not, of course, a vice. But the comfort of being well-fed can become more than merely physical. It can become the means by which we try to ease emotional and spiritual pain. We are gluttonous in different and highly individual ways. Mrs. X simply eats all the time, trying to satisfy her longing for companionship, while Mrs. Y is so addicted to gourmet dishes that people dread having her as a dinner guest. Mr. A drinks too much at parties, because he enjoys the attention he gets as the "life of the party." Mr. B, on the other hand, spends more money than he should on his wine cellar. (It should be noted, perhaps, that alcoholism is not the same thing as gluttony. It is a disease.) One of the vicious side effects of gluttony is that it can be fatal. When the physical vices become truly habitual, they frequently turn out to be fatal: the social drinker who indulges his or her taste for booze to the point of excess risks disaster on the highway. And, of course, whatever comfort we get from indulging our appetite is only temporary.

Lust is the distortion of another physical attribute. It is the attempt to solve all our problems by means of self-centered sexual activity. It ranges all the way from prudery to promiscuity, from morbid attention to other people's sexual behavior to morbid attention to our own. We need love as a plant needs sun; and lust is a substitute for love. We were, to be sure, created with sexual attributes, so that sex is part of our humanity. But in lust our sexual drives take on dimensions that have nothing to do with love or sex. Sex takes on all kinds of non-sexual connotations. It makes us feel important or grown-up. It makes us feel needed. It builds up a bruised ego. It becomes a means of brutalizing others. It turns into an act of rebellion against others or a means of inducing guilt in others. It can, given the burden of original sin, turn into an insatiable craving. The problem of lust goes back to our inability to overcome our estrangement from our selves and each other: "Then the eyes of both Adam and Eve were opened, and they knew that they were naked." (Gen. 3:7) What ought to be innocent and natural is not, and we can't seem to get back to the innocence, however many times we tell ourselves that there's nothing wrong with sex. The so-called sexual revolution of recent decades is not the cause of lust. It is merely symptomatic of our unhappy realization that human sexual behavior is askew, and of our desperate wish to get back to the state of innocence symbolized by the garden of Eden.

The other four traditional categories of vices are usually more difficult to describe than are those which derive from our physical attributes. Their origins are less specific and their outward signs less commonly condemned.

Anger is one. Essentially, anger is a distortion of our instinct for self-preservation and for preservation of those we love. If we imagine a grizzly bear, either wounded herself or fighting for the life of her cub, we can appreciate the extent to which the instinct we perceive as anger has its roots in our natural condition. But something happens when the instinct for preservation is linked with self awareness. What is natural in animals turns into something far more long-lasting, far more destructive, and far more addictive in human beings. We translate the "fight for life" into the "fight for self," and the results are frequently lethal. We hurt each other, for one thing. (Or, if we have been taught that anger is bad, we turn our anger inward and hurt ourselves.) Anger turned outward leads to all sorts of difficulties, ranging from prison sentences to corrosive remorse. Yet not all of us have short tempers or hasty tongues. Some of us are merely sulky and sullen. Some of us are irritable all day, never unleashing the anger inside. Some of us are sweetly critical of everyone and everything. The variations are endless, because they are so personal.

Anger is a feeling that we all share, because it is a response to fear. We have found ouselves alone, out of step with the world around us, as vulnerable as babes in the wood. This is a fearful state to be in, and the human response is the emotion of anger. It is when anger moves from emotion to action, from feeling to behavior, that the intrusion of self-centering twists it into vice. Suppose a good friend has let us down. The fact that he or she *is* a friend makes the feeling of anger more acute: we need our friends. Or suppose someone undercuts us at work. We find ourselves being righteously indignant, fighting back in our own angry way, because we have to have jobs in order to eat, because the *I* in all of us craves attention. In Genesis, Cain murdered Abel because Abel seemed to have won God's approval. Most of us would not go quite that far for God's endorsement; but all of us know how murderous we can get, how much of our energy is spent in anger that goes beyond the natural response to fear.

Covetousness is the effort to fill our emptiness by means of material possessions. It has very little to do with the real use of its objects or with actual physical security. Material things in the world around us are not wicked or bad, in and of themselves. We do have to have shelter and clothes and money, since we live in a physical world. However, there is often little correlation between what we need and what we *think* we need. As we look around us, we can see all kinds of things to be needed: a bigger TV set, a car, the latest technological wonder toy, a nicer house, and so on. Most of all, money. Money will buy the things that, we hope, will make us happy, secure, and peaceful. How much money do we need? We like to tell each other that we don't want much, just enough to get by on. Yet "enough to get by on" changes as our circumstances change. Furthermore, our deep-rooted terror of the future makes it important that we have enough for the future as well as the present. To complicate matters even more, we have acquired the notion that we can be popular, important, loved, if we have lots of money in the bank. Hence, we keep up with the Joneses if we possibly can, no matter who our personal "Joneses" are. We envy them their place in the scheme of things.

Covetousness is one vice that does not usually bring down as much disapproval on us as do many of the other vices. For one thing, trying to gather as many material possessions as possible is not frowned on in American society, unless gathering includes looting a riot-stricken area. Quite to the contrary, the millionaire who turns himself or herself into a billionaire is admired, provided the process is not considered illegal. Nor are we ourselves blamed for many of our more covetous activities—unless, of course, we get into trouble with our credit cards and go bankrupt.

But there is a dark side to covetousness, even in a highly materialistic society. We are really coveting something that isn't material at all. Money buys more than housing and clothes and TV sets. It buys power over people. It buys laws, governments, even preachers. Since we do not covet money for itself, or material possessions for their intrinsic worth, we have to examine what it is we really are in search of. Only as we discover the kind of security and well-being we are trying to catch and hold, do we find that possessions are substitutes, and inadequate substitutes at that.

Jealousy is the worship of other human beings, the attempt to find solutions for pain in the possession of people. So acute is our need for the love of others and, although we rarely think about it, for the love of God, that we clutch others to us with as much single-mindedness as a miser clutches his gold or a drowning man his life jacket. One of the more pernicious effects of being "sundered" from each other is that we can no longer be sure of love, and yet we cannot live without love. Consequently, we find ourselves depending on those we dare not let go. All of us share in the problem of belonging and loving, so we are all jealous to some extent. We very early acquire the habit of treating those around us as if *they* were the answers to *our* needs, as if they were pieces of property or pets or emotional convenience stores, catering to our whims. We use people to fulfill needs that go far beyond the need for love: we want to own their time, their abilities, and their personal lives. We like to tell them what to do and how to behave, not simply because we know better than they, but because by controlling what they do, we think we control them.

It is clear that parents, children, husbands, wives, lovers, and friends cannot do for us what we so often demand of them.

People fail us, when we put them in the position of having to provide us with perfect love. For one thing, nobody is perfect. For another, the more we demand, the less capable we are of giving love and the more badly we behave. Sooner or later, those we most value, on whom we most depend, get away from us, leaving us to our solitary misery.

Pride is generally considered as the inescapable vice. It is referred to as either the root of all other vices or as the most deeply ingrained. Pride is the indulgent concern for self over concern for God or each other. Pride is the perversion of our individuality, our sense of self respect and personal identity. These ordinary, natural elements of our personality become tools with which we try to solve our internal and external conflicts. Since our pain is personal, we attempt to alleviate it by our own personal methods. As in the case of the other vices, pride comes in all shapes and varieties. Vanity is a fairly obvious form: seeing ourselves in our own mirrors, we pride ourselves on our accomplishments, although those accomplishments may owe more to the work of others than to our own efforts. Hurt feelings are another clear signal, particularly as they are displayed to attract attention. Self-pity is easily recognized—in other people. So is self-righteousness, a form of pride which is always annoying in others, but rarely perceived in ourselves, especially when we have cloaked it in "religious" terminology.

Like covetousness, pride is not necessarily a social embarrassment, although in some of its habitual forms it tends to annoy other people. Since we learn as children that extreme forms of self pity or vanity are considered bad form, we usually dress pride up for public consumption. Thus, while we are feeling sorry for ourselves, we present ourselves as martyrs, a far more acceptable adult role than is that of the whiner. The tactic of disguising pride as something else does have its dangers, however. If we persist in seeing ourselves not as we are, but as we wish we were, we soon lose the capacity to see anything clearly. And as we judge events by their effect on us, we lose the vision of events as they really are. In this regard, we are like children who never grow up: a child whose family is broken by divorce can only perceive his or her loss, and therefore cannot understand the adult problems and pain that brought about the divorce. So it is with the adult who, thinking himself or herself to be God's gift to the business world, wakes up one day to find himself or herself jobless. Pride, like a fun-house mirror, distorts our vision of the way things really are. It enables us to set ourselves up as the moral and ethical standards of everyone around us, without ever noticing facts or history or our own contribution to the state of things.

Vices get us into all kinds of trouble. The glutton damages his own body. Families walk in mortal terror of the hot-tempered. People cross the street to avoid those who whine. It takes very little observation and thought to show us the numbers of occasions during which we find ourselves trapped by the effects of one or another of the manifold variations of pride. What do we do about it?

Probably the most common response is one of *flight*. We simply evade the implications of our behavior, either by placing the responsibility for our own vices on someone or something else—the sad state of the bank balance, the insensitivity of others, the neighborhood, or what have you—or by denying that our vices are what they are. Since we can't seem to stop behaving the way we do, other people and the world around us will simply have to change. And if they won't, we can always think positively about our failures. Thus, if we are gluttonous, we can make a virtue of good eating or heavy drinking. If we are slothful, we make a virtue out of getting away with cheating on a test or taking sick pay when we're healthy. If we are lustful, we boast about it. If we are jealous, we make a religion out of mother love or the sanctity of the home. If we are covetous, we not only judge others by the amount of money they have, but we talk about miserliness as if it were thrift. If we are angry, we commit murder on other people by trying to reform them, or we make cut-throat competition an acceptable practice. Pride becomes, by a strange about-face, the most admirable virtue: we become snobs, finding so much righteousness in ourselves that we are convinced God loves us more than anyone else.

This flight from the true nature of the vices scarcely ever works out well. We are never preserved from the consequences of our behavior simply because we have managed to justify them to ourselves. Other people can quite easily perceive what we refuse to look at, and besides, deep within us, we know that we are not made happy by running away from ourselves.

Another, less pleasant, method of dealing with our vices probably arises from self-disgust or from self-blame. When we get sufficiently sick of our behavior, we try to *fight* back. We try to improve ourselves. We resolve never again to drink that much, never again to say such hurtful things to those we love, never again to feel sorry for ourselves. Or, more realistically, we resolve to try to do better. For varying lengths of time, our efforts at fighting our vices may show results. Some of us can shed bad habits, for instance, can learn to control our tempers or to eat sensibly.

Yet even as we manage to fight one vice or one form of a particular vice, others seem to take over. We manage to control our tempers only to find that we are sorry for ourselves because no one understands how difficult our battle is. We have altered our eating habits and no longer behave like gluttons, but we are so proud of our achievement that we are now gossiping about the gluttony we observe in others. Indeed, just as we think we have our vices under firm discipline, we succumb to attacks of vanity that are fully as destructive as the vices we no longer exhibit. The fight against the state we are in is foredoomed, because our vices are only the outward signs of that inner sickness we cannot cure by ourselves.

And so we *despair*. We stop trying. When we reach the point at which we recognize our helplessness, we convince ourselves that there really is no hope either for us individually or for the whole human race. Despair shows up in many forms, most frequently in the kind of depression which permeates every aspect of our lives and haunts our happiest moments. Then there is the despair which surfaces as cynicism. We can find no good in ourselves, so we find no good anywhere around us. If someone else seems successful or happy or free, we are sure there is a dark and ugly secret behind all that outward goodness. Or, more ominously, there may emerge the despair which results in self-destruction. It hardly needs to be said that despair is no more a solution to our situation than is flight or fight.

What kind of help do we need, then? If nothing we do makes any significant difference, where do we turn?

One common assumption is that we need to be told what is wrong with us. In a way, we do: until we appreciate the extent to which our lives are warped by original sin, it is unlikely that very much of anything will happen to make us better. Unfortunately, knowledge of what is wrong with us does not, in and of itself, change us. If it did, we would not, after centuries of exploration into the ways and means of human existence, be in the same situation as our ancestors. Furthermore, the notion that all we need is self-understanding presupposes that if we understood ourselves, we could change. This is a little like assuming that all we need is an adjustment of the faults in our working parts, as if we were car engines in need of new spark plugs. Quite clearly, something more than knowledge is required.

When it comes to our vices, we like to think we need someone to tell us what to do, a sort of celestial Dear Abby, to whom we could tell our troubles and from whom we could get recipes for peace of mind. The problem here is that the best of advice has a way of never exactly fitting individual circumstances. Either it demands more of us than we can manage, or it confirms what we already suspect to be true. It does not restore us to the innocence of the garden of Eden.

Do we need comfort and solace? Nothing is more soothing than the thought that somewhere there is someone or something to take the burden from us. Yet nothing is more dangerous. It may be entirely appropriate for a father or mother to "kiss the hurt and make it well." But for another human being to tell us that sin is really only a temporary hurt is to deny the reality of our pain. It does no good to a sick man to tell him he isn't really sick, just as it does no good to tell a man trapped in the hell of anxiety that he must look at the "bright side"—if he could, he wouldn't be in hell.

Sometimes we think we need a good example, someone to show us the way. If only there were a mode of living that manifestly displayed what human life could be, we might be able to imitate that example and find rest. There are three traps in this idea. First, a good example is always someone other than ourselves, someone with different talents, different abilities, different problems. We can observe him or her with admiration, even envy; but no good example ever really shared out personal despair. In the second place, a good example nearly always frustrates our best intentions by succeeding where we fail. This is the difficulty many Christians face whenever they try to imitate the lives of the saints. Francis of Assisi was luminously happy in his life—but when we try to imitate him, we find the going very rough indeed. Good examples all too often prove to be irritating, rather than inspiring. If a saint can do it, why can't we? The question echoes what we remember from childhood: if little cousin Susie can tie her own shoes, why can't you? The burden of sin is back with us, as it always was.

Do we need to have our lives taken over and whipped into shape by someone more intelligent, more knowledgeable, more powerful than we? Someone to make our decisions for us? Someone to protect us from ourselves? This is the most tempting option of all. It also is the one most of us choose, once we find ourselves tired of fleeing, worn out from fighting, and deeply despairing. If we can find an external framework or order to which we can commit our lives, at least we no longer need feel responsibility for the dis-order that characterizes the human situation. Unfortunately, the imposition of external order does not touch the chaos of internal conflict, as the history of nations and the history of many religious cults demonstrate.

Quite simply, the greatest of all human needs—greater than the list we have already looked at—is for help that will straighten out what is wrong in the heart of us. And so, to each of us, sooner or later, comes the moment in which we take our first real steps in our journey in faith.

Finally, we cry out for a savior.

THREE

Redemption

Religions are supposed not only to provide explanations for our human condition but also to offer solutions. The word "religion" derives from the Latin for "to tie back" or "to tie together." Thus, whatever religion we subscribe to, even if it is the religion of atheism, the scientific method, or Marxism, or even "eat, drink, and be merry," we all are hoping that the fundamental division within us as individuals, and among us as a race, is being overcome.

From our religions we get a variety of answers to the problems we have identified. "Self-improvement" or "betterment of mankind," for instance, are widespread solutions, offered by religions all over the world, in different disguises. The basic premises are always the same. If we can juggle the social order, alter the economic traditions, improve what's amiss in the brain, we can cure the human race of all its tragic ills. Or, when we observe the limitations of this tactic, we can adopt a different premise; that it is such a hopeless situation, this business of being human, that the only religion that makes any sense is to live for the day, grab whatever pleasure we can find, and try to forget the rest. Neither of these religious premises really works in practice. Indeed, these attempts to tie ourselves together are merely the familiar responses of fight and despair raised to the level of conscious opinion.

Organized religions (*i.e.* systems of belief and worship that we ordinarily think of when we are using the word "religion") offer answers that are based on the premise that something very deeply ingrained is the source of our pain, and that neither rearranging our environment nor giving in to despair touches that source. There are organized religions that teach us that flight is our only hope, that we should do our best and wait for death to release us to a less difficult state. We are sometimes told that the world—and the flesh—are contemptible or illusory or evil. Many religions present us with the figure of the devil as a power responsible for everything that's wrong with us and invite us to do battle with "him," to fight *and* take flight from responsibility at the same time. Organized religions provide us with laws and rules of life which, if scrupulously obeyed, will give us a safe way to exist as well as the conviction that we are right in what we do and how we think, no matter what. They also give us comfort and a respectable way in which to take flight from the world and our selves.

We are accustomed to think of Christianity as being much the same as all other organized religions, just one of several world-wide systems of belief. Does it not hold out heaven as a reward for good behavior (fighting the "good" fight), or as an escape from the pain of existence? Does it not provide us with rules of life that will ensure that what we do is right? Does it not offer us a haven of peace?

To many non-Christians, Christianity looks very much like a religion of flight from the realities of scientific thought and social injustice. And to many others, both Christian and non-Christian, Christianity is so much a part of the fabric of the world we live in, that we can scarcely disentangle it from what we call Western civilization, the civilization we have so much trouble living in. Furthermore, we have even more trouble figuring out what it does offer us that is any different from whatever solutions we have devised for ourselves without religion. Perhaps this is why the central figure of Christianity—Jesus of Nazareth—is such a mystery to us.

What does Jesus of Nazareth look like, to us? Unhappily for us, we usually think of him in terms of the very answers to sin and vice that have already been tested and found wanting. To most people, he appears to be primarily a judge—an ethical leader who tried to free his people from meaningless restrictions or social injustice. Or perhaps we see him as the ultimate idealist, someone who presented us with laws of so lofty a nature that no one (except him) ever has been able to live up to them. Many Christians think of Jesus as a comfort in times of trial: he takes away—or ought to take away—our pain, if we can believe the hymns we sang as children.

Of course, he is a supreme example to the entire human race. If we patterned our lives after his, everything would be fine. (It should be noted, of course, that few of us would volunteer to pattern our deaths after his.) Then again, at Christmas, Christians and many non-Christians sing about Jesus as "the Savior"; but most would be hard-pressed to explain what the term "Savior" means.

The question we sometimes find ourselves asking is "So what?" We find it difficult to make any connection between the bits of information we have picked up about Jesus and the straits we find ourselves in. We certainly cannot easily perceive how he can help us with our vices or how he can heal our internal and external divisions. Perhaps the easiest way to discover what difference Jesus makes in the lives of those who journey in faith, is to look at the difference he made in the lives of the early journeyers, his followers.

The one thing that can safely be said about the people who followed Jesus of Nazareth, given what we know from historians and archaeologists, is that they were ordinary men and women, not "saints." They came from different backgrounds and had different jobs, but they were people much like ourselves.

For instance, most of the early followers were working people. Certainly, most of them were not aristocrats. They were religious people, good Jews, who wished earnestly to know God's will. They had grown up with a rich heritage both of laws and of rules of life and with a strong sense of community, despite the fact that they lived in what we would now call an "occupied" territory.

As the number of Jesus' followers increased, so did their variety. Some of them were scarcely "religious" people. Some of them were social outcasts. In fact, one of the shocking things about Jesus is that he did not turn his back on those who were "immoral." It is not recorded that he ever turned away anyone who really wanted to follow him, although there were those who could not bring themselves to give up their own solutions to pain even at his invitation.

As a group, the men and women who did follow Jesus cared greatly and passionately about the things which matter to all of us. They were not remarkable for their intelligence or education, but they were as human a group as ever assembled. Sometimes they behaved like squabbling children; sometimes they were astonishingly perceptive. A few of them would be successful leaders even today, but others would be as unacceptable socially now as they were then.

The questions they asked Jesus were the same questions people still ask: "Give us more faith"—"Let us see the Father and it will satisfy us"—"How can we know the way?"—"How often should we forgive our brothers?"

Yet while they were willing to follow him and ask him questions, they had no real understanding of the events they were involved in. It would be inaccurate to claim that his followers initially saw Jesus as anything other than someone like themselves, a man of very ordinary background. He was raised by a carpenter, to be a carpenter. Any extraordinary characteristics of his birth probably were not known to the Galilean fishermen who left their work to become his disciples. He ate and drank as other people did. He laughed and cried. He was, to be sure, a devout Jew, with a thorough knowledge of Jewish Law and of the heritage of his people.

Religious art has a habit of picturing him as a pallid, languid young man, looking incapable of doing anything more strenuous than sitting around in pious attitudes. But he was a Galilean peasant, and Galilee is a harsh land, even today. Life there was, and is, a struggle. In sum, Jesus was a true son of his land; otherwise his followers would never have taken his pronouncements seriously. And, to a surprising extent, the things he said were flavored by his origins. His stories were full of examples gleaned from real life, rather than from the abstract philosophy favored by other cultures.

He could be ironic or poetic, thunderously judgmental or quietly tender. He was for the most part disconcertingly quick with an answer; yet he could remain patiently silent in the face of extreme abuse. He was subject to the same sort of limitations and temptations which beset all human beings, as well as to the same physical pain which drives us to morphine. In sum, he was no sentimental idealist, but a personality of such power that the tough fishermen, the cynical tax-collector, the overworked housewife, the tired streetwalker, and all the rest found their lives altered by their association with him.

When he was about thirty, Jesus left the carpentry shop for the life of a wandering "rabbi" or teacher. This was not, in and of itself, particularly unusual. It often happened that adult Jewish men would feel called to go out into the world as teachers of the Law and its interpretations. These wandering rabbis were not "ordained" in the formal sense; nor were they priests, associated with the Temple in Jerusalem. Rather, they were something like lay preachers, more or less popular according to their skill in analyzing the many ramifications for daily life found in the rules of life embodied in the Old Testament.

Jesus' teachings were not, in and of themselves, shocking. Although he is commonly credited with having originated the Golden Rule, he did not. Almost all of his teaching can be found in the Old Testament, so that much of what he taught was familiar to his audiences. He told men and women to love God and neighbor, to seek out the things of God, to care for the sick and the poor, and, with some frequency, to repent. But he also spoke cryptically of an undefined state which he called the Kingdom of Heaven. His references to the Kingdom apparently had to do with something other than life after death, because he alluded to it as being "close at hand."

What gave Jesus' teachings their strange impact was the manner with which he spoke. "Truly I say to you..." prefaced so many of his remarks that the phrase took on the weight of serious authority. As his reputation spread, it was inevitable that his implicit claim of authority would be challenged. Yet even when directly attacked for the certainty with which he spoke—and acted—he turned back the questions put to him with a sure knowledge of all the implications hidden in them. Those who related the accounts of his life and teaching (the Evangelists) described him as "knowing what was in" people's hearts, as being able to reach beyond the obvious to the real. The effect was, of course, both dazzling and unnerving.

A great many people were attracted by Jesus' teaching and preaching. Although Judea was then only a very minor province of a very large Roman Empire, and although those who made up the crowds around Jesus were probably primarily very plain and ordinary people, it did not take long for him to attract attention beyond the immediate neighborhoods into which he went. He had collected about him twelve close associates (the Apostles), as well as a number of devoted admirers, but he also had gained a more widespread reputation, especially after he began healing the sick.

Faith healers have always been part of the human scene. They are still with us. Jesus, in a manner that somehow seems almost matter-of-fact, went about the countryside healing the fevered, the mentally ill, the paralyzed, and the leprous. Lepers may have been among his most notorious cases, since they were exiled from all human contact as being "unclean".

Accounts of his ministry give us the impression that the disciples accepted the healing miracles with little fuss. In fact, they brought the sick to him without fanfare. Again, they seemed not to comprehend the effects of his words and actions. Even as he asked that those who were healed keep quiet about what had happened to them, his fame was spreading. More and more people began to seek him out, to crowd around him.

Then there were other, far more mysterious demonstrations of Jesus' power. From whatever source, Jesus had the ability to dominate the forces of nature to a degree that terrified his disciples. They were bewildered and humbled by the figure who could calm a storm at sea, who walked on water, and who, even more significantly, recalled the dead Lazarus to life. To make a rational connection between this figure and that of the teacher and friend required a level of understanding that the disciples did not at first possess.

As the months went by, however this man became increasingly the center of the disciples' lives, and they became more and more conscious of his authority over them. It was not an authority imposed on them; rather, it was part of a relationship they freely undertook, attracted by their sense that there was something "different" about this teacher, something quite unlike the usual religious leaders and teachers. Like children, they assumed that he would care for and direct them all their days.

If his followers accepted the unsettling things that Jesus was saying, the nation's religious leaders began to consider him more than a temporary nuisance, more than just another itinerant preacher. If we look at the political condition of Judea at the time of Jesus' ministry, we can see why his air of authority quickly stirred up trouble. Judea in those days was an occupied country—something like Afghanistan today. A foreign power was in control, with puppet kings to mask the bitter fact that the Jewish nation no longer had independent existence. While the people were allowed to practice their religion (the Roman governors were pragmatic enough to see that religious persecution would make civil government more difficult), they had lost their glory as a people. Consequently, all Jews with any sense of history dreamed of the day of liberation, when the Son of Man, the Christ, the anointed one, the leader promised by the prophets, would deliver them. This longed-for leader was the Messiah. And Jesus of Nazareth bore a strong resemblance to the promised Messiah. He certainly acted with all the magnetism and power of a true leader. He could sway the crowds, he could do miracles, and He made public statements implying that he claimed the title.

If Jesus *was* the Messiah, however, he was not the kind of Messiah who would bring any comfort either to the men who governed Judea, or to the religious leaders who, in order to protect their religious settlement with the Romans, had accommodated themselves to the Roman Empire. To understand the violent emotions that he aroused in the hearts of those in power, we need to understand what they saw so clearly.

Judaism and its traditions encompass a vast knowledge of God, acquired over centuries of religious thought and experience. Among the facts that Jews for countless generations had lived and died for were two key insights into the relationship between human beings and God. First, there is only one God and He only is to be worshiped. Second, only God can forgive sin and bridge the gap between God and humanity. Indeed, forgiveness was the solemn high point of Temple worship. On the Day of Atonement, the high priest entered a tiny room at the heart of the Temple, the Holy of Holies set apart for God. There, and on this day only, he begged forgiveness for the nation.

Nowadays we take forgiveness much as we take aspirin, without thought for its power or its origin. Consequently, we find hard to comprehend the shock felt by the Jewish priesthood when Jesus claimed the power to forgive sins of pious Jews. The only analogy that works for us today is political and therefore misleading. But we might compare the priesthood's assessment of Jesus to how we would see a leader of persuasive power greater than any of our official leaders: as long as such a person keeps modestly within the area of "inspiration" or uplifting speeches, we would be content. But suppose that a highly attractive leader begins to make claims that are contrary to all that we hold dear? Suppose his followers begin to talk about him as knowing more than our government does, as being able to interpret the Constitution more accurately than our courts, our Congress, and our President? We might indeed find ourselves talking about shutting this person up, in the name of law and order and the American Way.

Hence the hierarchy's mistrust of Jesus. Their suspicions were confirmed when he committed blasphemy. He referred to himself as "one with the Father," which may not sound so terrible to us, but which sounded like—and *was*—a claim that struck at the heart of Judaism's understanding of God. Blasphemers were not just naughty people who ought to have had their mouths washed out; they were worse than murderers and thieves, because they broke the most sacred of all commandments: "You shall have no other gods before me." (Exodus 20:3) Even among those who may have admired Jesus grudgingly, the certainty grew that he was becoming a public danger. Judea was a political tinderbox. If Jesus became the focus for a religious and political rebellion, it could mean only disaster. There would be Roman reprisals, a tighter noose around the country's neck, and more sorrow for the people.

Tensions in Jerusalem were at the breaking point when Jesus, knowing perfectly well that he was courting arrest, entered the city to the acclaim of huge crowds who treated him as if he indeed were the Messiah. The events that followed form the basis of the Christian solution to the human condition.

One of Jesus' disciples, one of the twelve chosen to be his Apostles, betrayed his whereabouts to the high priest for the princely sum of thirty pieces of silver. The man who claimed kinship with God was arrested as a criminal. In the terror of the moment, his disciples deserted him. Jesus was taken by the Temple guards, put on trial hastily (and, it must be said, illegally) by the Jewish high council on charges of blasphemy, and turned over to the Roman civil administration to be put to death. The Romans could not have been less concerned about all this religious hairsplitting, but they, having allowed the Jews to practice their religion, were hardly in a position to step in. Of course, they too could perceive the political danger posed by Jesus, yet they chiefly were interested in keeping things peaceful. So they crucified him.

We are so familiar with this part of the story that we often forget that crucifixion was the most shameful form of punishment that could be inflicted on a Jew. The usual way of putting Jews to death was by stoning. Crucifixion was a disgusting death, reserved for those who had committed crimes that put them outside the community of Judaism. So the Jesus who had been hailed by the crowds as the Chosen One was cast out by being hung on a cross.

We also forget that Jesus was not a criminal, according to Roman law. His crime was one that neither they nor we see as wicked enough to warrant the death penalty, let alone this particular death penalty. Hence the cynicism with which he was treated by the Roman soldiers who whipped him and crowned him with thorns. As for the crowds, they either melted away—just one more good man, after all, scarcely the Messiah—or they taunted him: "Save yourself, and come down from the cross!" (Mark 15:30) And sorrowing both for Jesus' suffering and (acutely) for their own, the disciples hid from the scorn and fury of the mobs and the Temple guards. It was all over for them. Jesus was dead, and so was whatever about him had given meaning and purpose to their lives.

On the first day of the week after his death, some of the women who had loved him most went to the tomb where his body was buried in order to perform the traditional burial preparations. Because the day after his death was the Sabbath, during which all work was prohibited, they had not been able to anoint his body as the law prescribed. It was only as they were on their way that it ocurred to them that they had no way of getting into the tomb, which was a cave carved out of solid rock and closed up with a great stone place there so as to protect the body from desecration either by the mob or by the Temple guards. Whatever their feelings—that they would be unable to do this last service for the dead—their distress was converted into confusion when they arrived at the tomb. The rock had already been rolled to one side, and Jesus' body was gone.

A young man was there, as if waiting for them. He said, "Don't be afraid. You are looking for Jesus of Nazareth, who was crucified. He has risen, he is not here." The women ran back for help to the apostles. Two of the men came to investigate and found that the tomb was indeed empty, although the burial clothes were undisturbed.

Then, before the day was out, Jesus himself appeared among his frightened disciples. His body was changed but it was indisputably the body of Jesus, tangible wounds and all. Something beyond their comprehension—and ours—had happened. A man had died and had come through death not as a "spiritual entity" or a ghost, but in a resurrected state.

For forty days he appeared among them, randomly, at unexpected places and times, talking with them, reassuring them, teaching them as before, but with, we can be sure, a totally new effect. In one way, these were familiar encounters: his style of speech, for instance, had not changed. But in another way it was an entirely new situation. The resurrected Jesus spoke with an authority far greater than he had ever used. He was no longer the itinerant preacher and healer, no longer the carpenter, but a totally new being, at least new to them. It was a time of wonder and awe. Then, after forty days, he left them. His leaving is pictured in the accounts as an ascension into the heavens, holding to the Jewish tradition of God's abode as being above the skies. No matter how this ascension actually took place, his resurrected body withdrew from their sight. It was no longer possible for the disciples to think of him simply as their Master. He had removed himself from the limits of time and geography, leaving behind both a promise and a command that they be witnesses to the world of what had happened.

It is possible that more words have been written about, and more arguments stirred up by, the Resurrection and its consequences than have attended any other single event in world history. People have fought wars and made peace over the question of Jesus' identity. Western civilization as we know it was shaped by what emerged from the early Christian missions to the world. Nations and peoples were divided or united, according to various interpretations of what came to be called "The Mighty Acts of God."

Whatever we think of the historical consequences of what happened in Jerusalem long ago, one fact of timeless importance remains: it is from those events that Christianity takes its claim that human beings like us can live fruitfully and even victoriously within our human tragedy.

The men and women who had followed, deserted, and returned to Jesus now regarded him, and themselves, in the light of a totally new understanding both of his nature and of their own. Jesus no longer was just a good and holy man, a prophet, an earthly Messiah. He was (in some fashion still unclear to them) also God in human flesh. The things he had said to them, thereby were said by God. The deeds he did were God's deeds. The kinds of questions they had been accustomed to ask him now seemed irrelevant, even foolish. In *his* name they were to transmit the good news about him to "all nations", to forgive as they had been forgiven, to heal as they had been healed, to teach as they had been taught.

Because succeeding generations weren't there at the time, there has always been much speculation about the Resurrection. Much of the speculation is pointless, since it seems to derive either from our reluctance to face this challenge to our own self-created answers to the human condition or from our profound misunderstandings of that condition.

To a great many people, the idea of the crucifixion itself is offensive. Moslems, for example, share the old Jewish abhorrence of such a shameful death. We still hear repeated the same question asked at the foot of the cross: "If he is the Son of God, why didn't he come down from the cross?"

For other people, the Resurrection is either a scientific impossibility or a fairy tale. Some regard the whole idea as irrelevant in our lives: we can accept the Resurrection as sweetly symbolizing the awakening of spring in the earth, as roughly significant as the Easter bunny, but not as the supreme impact of God's power over death.

To some, however, the Resurrection is the most important thing that ever happened. The same fishermen, social outcasts, and ordinary folk who had been so maddeningly slow to get the point of Jesus' teachings were the first ones to see the implications of his death and Resurrection, perhaps because they had been so quick to abandon him when he was arrested. They began openly, and without fear, to preach about him. Knowing perfectly well that they themselves were courting death by doing so, they went about Judea proclaiming the (then) shocking news that the crucified Galilean carpenter was the Son of God. They called him Lord (not at all the same thing as "Master"), which was blasphemy. They forgave sins, which was in some ways worse, since it led other Jews into blasphemy. They healed the sick. They called on the Jewish people to repent, to believe that God's kingdom had come to pass. And they won convert after convert, despite all efforts to halt them. Some of them died as martyrs.

Looking at them, even from this distance, creates in us a sense of envy. Their association with Jesus had changed their fear and foolishness into full assurance and conviction. They knew something—had witnessed something—that, as it turns out, we would all like to know. What was it?

At first, they knew one fundamental fact only: the Son of the living God, the Christ, had been walking the hills and plains of Judea with them. This knowledge gave incalculable importance to the things he had said and done. For one thing, he had called them away from their old lives to follow him, offering them "newness" of life. For another, he had taught them about God's realm or kingdom, that God does not rule the lives of men and women in the same manner that human rulers do, that what human beings regard as important—wealth, status, power—is of no value in the eyes of God, that "the last shall be first." For yet another, he had taught them and shown them in healing miracles that God forgives human sin before the sinner is even aware of the need for forgiveness. The kind of life they had lived with him was not only of this world, but was somehow also eternal, and the Kingdom of Heaven (a phrase probably interpreted at first either in terms of politics or in terms of life after death) is *now*, not later. Entering this kingdom depends on a quality of life called faith, specifically faith in Jesus, whatever that might mean.

These statements abot the kingdom of God, made in a variety of ways, both in sermons and in stories, make it clear that the Kingdom is the opposite of the sin-self-governed existence human beings must endure, that the disciples themselves had endured. It is clearly not a restoration to the natural state of the Garden of Eden. Rather, it derives from a new relationship with the Lord God. Not all the disciples were particularly concerned about the logic behind the Kingdom. They were far more concerned with living in it and telling other people about it. But in the telling, and in the development of a community of those who had faith in the risen Jesus, certain convictions about the meaning of "the mighty acts" emerged and were given shape in the teachings and writings that the apostles circulated.

The most obvious conclusion is that Jesus had overcome death, not in some hazy future, but physically and concretely.

More significantly, he had not overcome death simply on his own behalf, as if God were concerned only about God. On the contrary, Jesus, the Christ, had returned to them, to the same human race that had rejected, shamed, and killed him, demonstrating a kind of divine love that is beyond human imagination.

God's love for humanity was not a new idea, of course. The prophets had known long ago that the God of power was also a God of love. But that God would bother with humanity to this extent was a new insight: God becoming one of us, dying because of us, then coming back to us. For the disciples, the effect was one of transformation. How did it feel to have deserted the God-Man as he was murdered, and then to have found that God's love had pursued them even while they shivered in their hiding places? Their own sin was overcome, as death was.

Another conclusion is that once sin and death have their stranglehold broken, they never again can have the same power over us. Our consciousness of our selves does not evaporate, and our vices continue to plague us; but since the basic relationship between humanity and God has been altered, we are free to be obedient again. What we could not do for ourselves, He did for us.

Still another conclusion, obvious to the early Christians but less so to us, is that Jesus' death amounted to the perfect sacrifice to God. Sacrifice is not exactly a familiar note in contemporary thought, but the idea of restitution or atonement is. In most religious traditions, it is customary to make offerings of the best or the most important, as a means of making up for failures and offenses. The same principle applies in everyday life. The criminal must sacrifice some of his life in prison. The tax evader must pay a fine. The quarrelsome must sacrifice his or her pride in order to apologize. But if self centered humanity wishes to make atonement to the God they have chosen to ignore or reject, what kind of sacrifice will do? Only the best, the most important of human beings would suffice. In the case of Jesus, the sacrifice was willing, indeed deliberate, and it was total, involving in one person both God and humanity.

There is very little said in the accounts of Jesus' ministry about the meeting of human needs or the solving of human problems. Indeed, after the Resurrection the needs seem to have changed shape. It is clear from the evidence that the disciples very quickly stopped talking about personal needs and problems. To those of them who had been asking the same questions we always ask, the questions no longer had any bite or force.

While it would be tremendously reassuring if we could read in the New Testament that the disciples instantly lost all their vices and lived happily ever after, they did not. They remained much the same sort of people. They had the same bodies and minds and limitations as always. They had to face the same sort of hopeless tedium as before. But there was a new kind of power, because they had known what it means to follow a Savior.

FOUR

Church

The unqualified Christian assertion—that Jesus' death and Resurrection give human beings victory over the fundamental disorder that causes our troubles—leaves many people dissatisfied, not to say skeptical. Our dissatisfaction does not necessarily grow out of refusal on our part to assent to the proposition that Jesus is God-Man. We can accept that proposition in a general way, and still not see what difference it makes. The "mighty acts of God" took place almost two thousand years ago. However convincing they may have been then, to those who were witnesses, they do not seem to have made any radical change in our personal lives today, let alone to the history of human misery in the intervening centuries. To be sure, we can see that many people have, through the centuries, been touched by the redemption and reconciliation that the disciples experienced. Indeed, in every generation individual Christians offer testimony that we are bound to hear. Unfortunately, we ourselves continue to struggle along with unsatisfied needs, messy problems, and painful questions, unable to grasp whatever saving power was and is available to some. Either there is something different about the "saints"—some hidden talent for "faith"—or else there is something still missing in our understanding of what happened to them.

Even the Christian Church, as an institution based on commitment to the risen Christ, does not seem as immediately important to us today as, by all the evidence, Jesus himself was to his followers. It makes no difference to what Christian group we belong, if any, because the same charge of irrelevance can be made against all. Despite the Church's official faith in Jesus Christ as Lord and Savior, thousands, if not millions, of Christians still seem to be looking elsewhere for redemption. Still more unsettling, the Church's activities through the centuries have all too often increased human misery, and were concerned with the kingdoms of *this* world, rather than the Kingdom of God.

We can trace part of our confusion to our view of what the Church is. Much of the time, we see it as an abstract formality, rather than as a collection of human beings just like ourselves. We accuse the Church of failing us, when we really mean to complain about individuals within the Church. Furthermore, because there are forms of government in all the varioius Christian communities, we confuse the structure of the Church with its job. There are countless examples in history of the Church acting out of the same confusion, so it is no wonder that the problem persists.

But there is more to our perception than this. We also seem to be asking that the Church provide us with the very kinds of "saviors" we have tested and found wanting in other places and among other communities. We are not seeking for Jesus among his people, but for salvation according to our own taste or inclination. It is sobering to realize that what most people seek in the Christian community is an endorsement, a blessing, in a sense a "christening" of the things, the ideas, and the relationships that characterize our own ineffectual attempts to reorder our disordered existence. We sometimes ask the Church, for instance, to be a sort of divinely endowed club, instituted to provide us with an antidote to acute loneliness. Or we talk about Church as a "family"—which in a sense it may be. But if that is all it is, all we will find in it are the same old family problems we are trying to get away from. Then again, from a despairing distance, we may assume that the Church is simply one more bureaucratic institution designed to take care of us or govern us, an institution that, like the school system or the federal government, touches our lives in ways that are all too often irritating, different from secular institutions only in that it is formally religious and therefore supposed to be better. To make matters worse, the Church is full of people suffering from all the vices we have been taught (sometimes by the Church) to avoid: hence the frequent accusation of hypocrisy. What is it, therefore, that we look for?

Some of us want very much for the Church to assume a sort of benevolent tyranny over human life. We want to be told exactly what to do, what to believe, what to pray, what to think, even what to read. In daily life, we subscribe to the ideal of political freedom. But when it comes to religious questions, we run from freedom as if it were the plague. There is a cozy sense of safety about an organized religion that is all-powerful, that claims it can *make* us happy. Furthermore, we feel secure within the company of those who see the Church's primary responsibility as that of reforming the world, of stamping out sin, or straightening out all those who intrude on our peace of mind. In other words, we want the Church to carry out for us, with (presumably) God's blessing, our instinct to fight in response to sin, to find us something or someone to blame for our predicament, to turn our anger into "righteous indignation."

Or we expect the Church to solve our problems for us. When things get bad, we turn to the pastor (who is generally thought of as a sort of professional Christian) or to a church-going neighbor or to the Bible for specific advice. We may or may not take the advice we get, but at least we ask for it out of the theory that the Church's job is to take from us the burdensome responsibility of choice and decision-making. If this is all we ask of the Church, it need hardly be said that we are going to be disappointed, if not in the kind of advice we get, then in the inevitable fact such advice has no real effect on what ails us.

We will be disappointed, too, if we think of the Church as a refuge from the tempests of life, a safe place to hide from pain, as if it divinely supported our flight from the reality of human sin. Church services, for instance, can provide us with the feeling of being soothed, as we hear the familiar hymns and prayers, and as we hide ourselves in the traditions and stability that the Church so often represents. Yet the notion that the Church is a means for escaping reality is loaded with problems, because we always find out, sooner or later, that the Church is no refuge from anything. There are just as many gossips, bores, and snobs in the Church as there are at the office. People can be just as greedy at a parish supper as they are at a restaurant. Furthermore, the Church is not changeless. A new pastor, a new hymn tune, a revised prayer, or a new building can take all the balm out of the services. If we move to a new town, a new church may jar all of our sensibilities. But even if we did manage to find a Church "home and family" in which no questions were ever asked and in which we got all the security and escape we asked for, our fundamental problem would not be solved. Flight from the "now" is no solution, because we still must live with ourselves.

Of course, we all expect the Church to set a good example. We are scandalized by the reports of "good Christians" who turn out to be embezzlers or cheats or scoundrels. We are shocked when our clergy (whom we expect to be "more" Christian than ordinary people) turn out to be less than perfect. We are honestly indignant when we read about corruption or political maneuvering in the Church—past or present. And the rancor that characterizes the behavior of some denominations toward others would lead us to suppose that Jesus taught a message of hatred rather than of love. Yet looking to the Church for a good example proceeds from the same fruitless assumption that looking for any good example has: even if we could find one, it would have little or no effect on us. If anything, good examples make our own flaws and failures more glaring. A perfect Church would have no room in it for human beings.

These are some of the demands we make of the Church. Essentially, we are asking that this institution, this community, these followers of Jesus treat the symptoms of sin, rather than the underlying causes. Consequently, we frequently cannot see any radical change in ourselves when we turn to it for help. To be sure, we find all of these demands being met, to a greater or lesser degree, in most Christian communities: they do provide order for much of our external disorder; they do help us with our problems, they do give us comfort and a sense of permanence; they do set examples for us. But—if this is all they do, then they still have not brought us into a relationship with the risen Christ.

So we have to ask whether the Church is supposed to be something more, or else we have to ask whether we should be looking at this company of believers in a different light.

If ever there were a group of people who were confused by events and unsure of what to do, it was that group of eleven men (eleven because the one who had betrayed Jesus had hanged himself) who were picked out by Jesus as his apostles. They were acutely aware that they had been witnesses to something of earth-shaking importance. They were also acutely aware that something had happened to *them*. Jesus had given them quite explicit instructions to go out and tell the world about the Kingdom of God. Even if he had not, they would scarcely have been able to keep this kind of news to themselves. People who have been healed of a terrible disease want to let other sick people know about the cure.

But when—and how—could they begin? How could a tiny band of ignorant and uneducated men communicate this kind of news to an indifferent, antagonistic, often hostile world?

Before his death, as well as in the interval between the Resurrection and his withdrawal from them, Jesus had made some significant promises: "These things I have spoken to you, while I am still with you. But the Counselor, the Holy Spirit, whom the Father will send in my name, he will teach you all things . . ." (John 25:1–2); and "But you shall receive power when the Holy Spirit has come upon you. . . ." (Acts 1:8) Then, ten days after he had left them, the promises were dramatically fulfilled. The Holy Spirit entered into the personalities of the assembled apostles, not only giving them the power they needed, but binding them together into a community which would come to be named the Church. The story, found in the Acts of the Apostles, sounds strange to many twentieth-century ears. It was definitely not an everyday occurrence.

The apostles had chosen a twelfth man to fill the place of Judas, and they were meeting to celebrate the Jewish holiday of Pentecost, when "suddenly a sound came from heaven like the rush of a mighty wind, and it filled all the house where they were sitting. And there appeared to them tongues as of fire, distributed and resting on each one of them. And they were all filled with the Holy Spirit and began to speak in other tongues, as the Spirit gave them utterance." (Acts 2:1–4) Not only could they talk to each other, but they now could talk to the world in languages that the world could understand.

The importance of Pentecost is not, despite its highly emotional flavor, the drama of the occasion. This was not a "sawdust trail" or a "born again" conversion experience for those who were there. The conversion experience had happened at Easter and during the forty days following the Resurrection. Rather, this invasion of the Spirit into the lives of the apostles enabled them to do what Jesus had told them to do. As God had entered the world of human beings in the person of Jesus of Nazareth, He now entered the lives of Jesus' followers. They were not, in fact, alone. Wherever they went and whatever happened to them, God the Spirit was with them. Now we can begin to perceive what the Church is supposed to be doing for and through us. What we find the apostles and disciples doing and saying, after Pentecost, is not exactly what we ourselves might expect, given what we usually think the Church is all about. Yet what they did—and said—converts our expectations.

They knew they had been called, even commissioned, to go out and tell people what had happened, to preach the message of repenting, to call others to seek the Kingdom of God. What they said could be paraphrased like this:

> The Kingdom of God is *now*. If you wait for it, it will never be yours. You will have to recognize the other saviors you have followed for what they are—agents of dis-

order, of flight, and despair. You must turn away from these. The only living Savior has come. Jesus, who died and rose from the dead, is the only Savior who can reconcile you with God. God has come to us, when we could not climb to Him. So put your faith and trust in Him. But you must not delay, for the present moment is what matters.

The apostles also knew that they had been forgiven for the sin that had divided them from God. They now went out into the marketplaces and the countryside to talk about forgiveness and to heal the sick and forgive the sin-sick:

You couldn't, of your own capabilities, do anything about the gulf which has separated you from God, so God has bridged the gulf for you. He has walked among us, He has willingly allowed us to kill Him, and He has come back from the dead to forgive what we have done. The Judge who passes sentence on us all has come down from His bench and has served out the sentence for us. Though you are afflicted with the same mortal sickness which was the death of us all, you can share in this forgiveness. All you need to do is to take it into your innermost heart.

Power to live within the tensions of this world had been communicated to the Church with the coming of the Strengthener. Now the apostles set out on their mission, passing to others the same power:

Come, take the power of God into your own life. This Church is like Christ's earthly body, the body that died and was raised. As He enables us to stand erect in the midst of persecution, torture, terror, and sorrow, He will do the same for you. God will graft you into this new physical body of Christ. He will come and dwell with you, as He has with us. By His power—not your own—you will be able to live in the Kingdom. Now your sin has separated you from God, from each other, and from your true self, and you are dying. We offer you new life. We offer, by the power of God the Holy Spirit, new birth and new being.

These are the elements of the Church's ministry, as the apostles and disciples saw it, and this kind of ministry distinguishes the Church from all other human groups.

What the Church provides has little appeal, unfortunately, when we are either reluctant to give up our current saviors or fail to recognize them for what they are. It makes us decidedly uncomfortable when we are called on to "repent" our sin, although all we really repent is the hurt it does us. We are even more uncomfortable when we find we can't save ourselves. What most of us would really prefer, if we could shop around for a savior, would be one who would tinker around with our lives, who would let us keep some of our treasured vices, who would offer not a new life but an improved one. The Church's real ministry will always seem a bit extreme to us, if all we seek is just a little help.

One of the most irritating statements made from time to time by the Christian Church is the assertion that there is no "salvation" for those outside its company. This claim seems outrageously arrogant. How can the Church be so sure it knows what God is up to? How can the Church be so unloving? There are billions of people who never had the opportunity to respond to Christ's call—natives in Africa, for example, and tiny babies who never lived to grow up. There are other billions whose own religions satisfy them, and who are we to say that God doesn't love Moslems and Hindus and Buddhists? And when we look around us at the Christians we know, members of the Church, they do not seem conspicuous for their saintliness. It is manifestly unfair that the Church claims "salvation" for these officially endorsed Christians, while denying it to much finer candidates who are not Christian.

Behind these objections, some of which develop out of the mistaken idea that "salvation" means "immortal life," there lies another, less altruistic notion, one that many of us share. We luxuriate in the firmly-rooted conviction that God the Holy Spirit could do a better job on us as individuals if we met Him in solitude, by ourselves. We are convinced (especially if we have read about Pentecost) that we can know God more intimately when the relationship is not cluttered up with the distractions of other people and Church customs and public worship. It is as if we would like the Holy Spirit to set us apart in a literal sense, to tailor "salvation" to our personal satisfaction.

The real question, of course, is whether the Church is necessary. When this question is asked out of serious concern for those who can never be part of the Church, the answer is obvious. We have no way of being absolutely certain that the Christian Church (or any one of its many branches, for that matter) is God's only means of reaching out to human beings. It seems plain that the apostles' message is not that Christians monopolize all God's attention, but that we can, if we wish, respond to *this* invitation, that we can choose to enter the Kingdom of Heaven now, that we can allow the Spirit to make us new. This does not mean that all those who never hear the call are automatically sent to hell. God's mercy is wider than we can know.

But the question about the Church's being necessary is sometimes asked out of our wish to establish our own grounds for redemption, to set our own rules for God's help. In this case, the answer is not so simple. For even while we know intellectually that we can never bridge the gulf separating us from God, it is extremely difficult to put away the familiar crutch of pride. The illusion of self sufficiency remains with us, under all our fine words and our concern for the souls of non-Christians.

We are forced back to the realization that the Church's ministry is unique, even if it is not perfect. Nothing else will do the job, because there is nothing else to do the job. We are aware only in moments of self-confrontation of the terrible extent of the human dis-order, and only on rare occasions can we face the facts of our own unhappiness. In most occasions we like to think we need a new job or a new love or a second chance. The only way in which we can confront the knowledge of sin is with the prior assurance of God's forgiveness, given us by those who themselves have experienced it and who have learned to face themselves—in short, by the Church. Individual religious experience is often truly uplifting. There is something indescribably fulfilling about our moments of solitary communion with God. Yet the dangers are clear. We are not alone. We are part of the human race. We cannot live out our lives in splendid isolation. When we elect to follow our own judgment, we run the risk of winding up in splendid nothingness.

One of the descriptions which seem to catch the character of the Church in a few words is a paraphrase of the name of another organization: the Church is a sort of "Sinners Anonymous." It affords help not from those who are perfect, but from those who have been where we are and who are themselves on the same journey that we are. The Church is in many respects a chain of very weak links—some shockingly so. It is not a hotel for saints, as we can see for ourselves. If it were, no unreconstructed human being would belong to it. Those who make up its communities are not recognizable by virtue of their saintliness. They only reach saintliness as God's power is made manifest in them, through their faith and through what they do.

The faithful have, in some way or other, heard the same call that the apostles and disciples heard. They have begun to perceive the beginnings of a change in the way in which they view the world around them and themselves, as if they could see through a new set of eyes. While nothing much has altered in their world, it looks different to them. They begin to find themselves empowered to cope with the problems and pain of existence. The problems and pain have not miraculously evaporated, to be sure; but their helplessness has been turned around and has become strength. For the most part, even the faithful see little that is dramatic about the change in themselves. Some may have experienced a sudden transformation, but the vast majority have not, because the "change of heart" happens deep within them. In fact, the change of heart (sometimes referred to as "conversion") can usually be recognized only in looking back, in comparing the old life with its old saviors and the new life under Christ. The Church to which they belong helps them identify what has happened to them. It both communicates the power of the Spirit and assists the faithful in recognizing the operation of the Spirit in their daily lives.

So, while on the surface of things, nothing could be less likely as a source of the transforming power of Jesus than the motley collection of ordinary human folk known as the Church, in point of fact it *is* the Church that brings that power to bear on the immediate human situation. Just as God made Himself known to the people of Judea in a carpenter—a physical, living, breathing person—so He makes Himself known to people of all generations in the physical, living, breathing people known as the Christian Church. St. Paul's analogy sums it up best: he wrote about the Church as "body of Christ" as if Christians were like cells in a human body, each with different tasks, but all given life by God.

What characterizes this "body of Christ"? Obviously the Church has a common Lord and Savior. This seems obvious enough. Yet, from all appearances, this Lord does not seem to be the same one in every branch of the Church or in every generation. Sometimes the Lord is depicted as an army general, leading troops of Christians off to war. Sometimes He is presented as a shepherd—and not a very real one, at that. Sometimes all we are shown is His suffering, as if Easter never happened. Sometimes the fact of His death is completely overlooked. What happens, of course, is that different Christian communities emphasize different aspects of their common Lord. Indeed, the emphasis of one denomination may grow out of the conviction that an important characteristic of the Lord has been overlooked, that some other characteristic of the Christ needs to be made known. For instance, if one group of Christians is pointing to that figure of a military leader as the Lord, some other Christians will resist that picture and show us the teacher who gave us instructions about humility and service. We have had all kinds of images of the Savior presented to us by the Church, but none of the images, we can be sure, *is* the Christ.

Because we are limited by our humanity, the Church in its entirety asks that we commit ourselves to one Lord without being quite able to perceive exactly all that pertains to His person. The divisions among Christians occur not because the Lord is different from place to place or time to time, but because Christians are different. The Church is referred to as *one*. But its unity, the gift of the Spirit, cannot be equated with uniformity. Rather, like our physical bodies, it has widely differentiated parts. Only the Christ we worship, and the Spirit we are filled with, remain the same.

Life within any community of the faithful is never exactly easy. There are, sitting next to us in a church service or at a parish supper, people we dislike, people we know to be less virtuous than we, people who annoy or invite disapproval, people (in fact) just like us. Then there are, up in the pulpit or at the altar, clergy who are themselves still grappling with their problems, clergy who are always preaching what they probably don't practice.

Furthermore, since Christian communities, like individual Christians, must live in a far from perfect world, they exhibit a tendency to take on characteristics that are far more worldly than Christian. Churches, then, get involved in all sorts of things that have little or nothing to do with what their Lord said and did. In one sense, the Church is, after all, only a slice of life, with all the headaches and problems that always accompany life.

But it is also something more. It is *holy*. That is, there is leaven not only in that lump of dough called St. Someone's Parish, but also in the various Christian groups, as well as the Church as a whole. The leaven is the Holy Spirit. Just as yeast makes bread dough grow and change shape, so the Spirit acts on ordinary human beings to form a body that grows and changes. He constantly intrudes in the life of the Church, challenging, shaping, unsettling, and forcing growth. Without the Spirit, the Church would be no more than one more institution of do-gooders. Instead, its life is that of God.

The faithful are primarily concerned with the present moment, because Christ's ministry is always directed to the here and now. Yet they are sustained—nourished, even—by the past, and the Church has a history that is as much a part of its substance as is the present. The Church is universal, it is *catholic*. (The word *Catholic* is sometimes used to denote one branch of the Christian community—the Roman Catholic Church.) Christian heritage provides not only a broad variety of traditions, but a vast accumulation of experiences, of tactics for dealing with human problems, of practical applications of Jesus' ministry.

But the Church is catholic in another sense, and when it appropriates to itself the term, it is referring to something more than its history. Its ministry is also universal, because the problem of human sin is not localized. Sin destroys not just the lives of a few sensitive people, but the lives of all. Furthermore, sin acts on the whole of each individual life; it is not confined to this vice or that. Hence, the Church concerns itself with the whole of human life, every area of existence. So it is catholic—universal—in its provision of ministry to all people and to all of the individual human being.

It would be an exaggeration to suggest that Christianity has to defend itself against the members of the Church. Yet is has seemed necessary from the very beginning to appeal to some kind of continuing authority, in order to keep the ministry of Christ from being turned into something else, into the ministry of this disciple or that preacher. The difficulty showed up very early indeed in the Church's history, and it continues to this day. In their enthusiasm, Christians sometimes seem to forget what they're really up to, to become so deeply involved in one aspect of Jesus' teaching, for instance, that they unwittingly throw away another. Consequently, the Church is *apostolic*. It traces its authority to speak and to minister back to the original apostles, the twelve who were commissioned by Christ and endowed with the Spirit at Pentecost.

Because it is apostolic in that historical sense, the Church is apostolic in another, perhaps more immediate fashion. The word itself derives from the Greek word for "messenger." As the original apostles were sent out to be messengers of Christ's death and Resurrection, to preach and teach and heal, so the Church is sent out as messenger, as a community of messengers, to bring the ministry of Christ wherever they are.

These four adjectives—one, holy, catholic, and apostolic—describe the Church as it is. Not all Christian groups subscribe to all four. Indeed, it could be argued that it is not always and everywhere one, or holy, or catholic, or apostolic. Still, the Spirit moves within it. The Christian community today, for instance, is actively moving toward a clearer demonstration of oneness, in the ecumenical movement. Christian groups are paying more attention to manifestations of the Spirit, both in theology and in worship. And groups that used to think the word "catholic" a symbol of terror or superstition have begun to understand its real meaning. There are clear signals too that the Church in general and Christian groups in particular are no longer content to sit about in what have been called "fur-lined foxholes." They are moving out to show forth the ministry of Christ in their daily lives as well as among the suffering around the world.

In the final analysis, however, most of us who are trudging wearily along on our personal journeys are still trying to get help for what ails us. Most of us aren't quite ready to feel apostolic, because we haven't quite got the message ourselves. What do we *get* from the Church?

We obviously get a lot from the services we ask for, even though they may have little or no effect on our deepest pain. We do get moral leadership, advice, counsel, refuge, and all the rest. We would get the same from any high-minded organization, whatever its mission. These services are, in a way, fringe benefits, nice to have but not life-giving. What the Church does offer is much more. It offers Christ's own ministry. Within its activities are to be found all the elements of teaching, prayers, sacrament, and community that characterized Jesus' work. It is, after all, the body of Christ on earth.

How we make use of the Church's ministry is, of course, largely up to us, just as it was up to the disciples and apostles in response to Jesus. We are benefited only to the degree that we ourselves respond. For instance, there is no use looking to the Church for the solution to all our problems, unless we are at the same time facing up to the real source of our pain. There is no refuge in the Church—unless we are prepared for the radical alteration of our lives from the inside. There is no security in this Community—except within the hidden foundation of the Spirit, and He moves in very mysterious ways.

Above all, of course, there is no communication to us of the saving, healing power of Jesus of Nazareth, unless we hear the call, accept the forgiveness, and welcome the strength to live within the Kingdom that He promised.

FIVE

Sacraments

For those who are journeying in faith, to accept Jesus of Nazareth as Savior is the equivalent of taking, in the words of the children's game, a "giant step," a step that requires the reorientation of our total existence. We are asked to turn around, to see ourselves with new vision, to examine the old, destructive means by which we have been coping with our lives, and to put these means aside. In view of the changes in store for us, the invitation extended by the Church, as Christ's Body, may seem compelling, only moderately attractive, or downright threatening. While the prospects offer us the help we want, they also seem to require of us a level of self-understanding and disciplined attention that we have so far not noticed in ourselves.

Indeed, answering Jesus' call turns out to be only the first in a series of "giant" steps. We are in effect being asked to learn to walk in a new direction untested by us, to proceed on our journey without a clue as to the accommodations available. At the same time that we face the radical rebuilding of our responses to life, we also face a new and untested relationship with God and with other people. How is all this to be managed?

Apart from acknowledging our own inability to make things right, apart from wishing to be forgiven and to be reconciled with ourselves, with others, and with God, there seems no way to move without the risk of making all the familiar human missteps. Old habits and problems die hard.

At no point does our human helplessness show itself more clearly than here. We want to be rescued from ourselves, but rescuing ourselves is something we cannot do. Past efforts in that direction have brought us nothing but grief. In fact, it seems that all we can do is sit around and wait for someone else to make the move for us. Having said "Yes" to Christ, we can do nothing more.

Ahead of us, another problem begins to emerge. The Church invites us to take the power of God into our lives. But doing that is not so simple as it sounds. We have been running for a long time—all our lives, in fact—on our own steam, on human energy, on human ideas, on human "religions." Much as we know that we can no longer continue to live in that fashion, we are afraid to put away the only things that have kept us going, not until we have personally experienced and tested some other kind of power. A drowning man may know that the water-soaked log he is clinging to is an inadequate life preserver. He may have been more than willing to yell for help and to welcome his rescuers. But he dares not let go of his log until someone throws him something better.

Although we are drawn to Jesus, one of the elements in his teaching is unavoidable. Out of our differing backgrounds, he calls us to live within the Kingdom of God. This call poses yet another difficulty. How, in this world, can we live in that Kingdom? Words and promises are all very well, but we have to deal with a world that bears little resemblance to the Kingdom he talked about, a twisted, distorted world, full of all sizes and shapes of hatred, pain, and injustice. If God's Kingdom were a political and economic reality, we might feel some certainty, some sense that we might have a chance for a new life. Yet the Kingdom, for better or for worse, is not of this world.

On the other hand, *we* are very much a part of the world. For us to deny this fact would be for us to deny our humanity. So wherever we are in our journey, people and events will continue to intrude on us. We still may lose a job or a loved one. Our children may continue to break our hearts, and our parents may continue to dominate us. We still cannot distinguish God's love from all the loves in our lives. We still scarcely know who we are. Short of running away from everything around us—becoming beachcombers on some South Sea island or hermits on some mountain top—we see no way for the Kingdom to make sense in our personal lives. How can we possibly enter on a new life, when we must continue to live in terms of the old? In sum, how can we be re-created, made over, when everything else stays the same?

Obviously, it would be easier for us if we were as fortunate as the disciples were. They were able to ask Jesus questions like these, to touch him, to watch him in action. Their world was not very different from ours, really, but they had God in the world with them, a circumstance that clearly made a significant difference. We have to cope with our questions without a physical, tangible, visible Savior. And so we look around us for something more than the Church's call. We look for something that will give us the conviction of God-in-the-world-right-now that the disciples enjoyed. When we get discouraged in our search, we sometimes say, "If only Jesus were alive today!" We don't quite realize that thereby we negate what we have already assented to, that is, our faith in the risen Christ. Our problem is that the price we see ourselves paying, as we answer the call, is the abandonment of our own efforts to manage life. It is an expensive price tag. The disciples had an advantage in that they knew to whom they could pay the price.

But when we begin to sort out the feelings underlying our nervous reluctance to give up our old saviors, we gradually become aware that there are two barriers to be faced. We need, first of all, something more than abstract ideas and promises. Of those we already have more than enough. We want to be turned around, because we don't know how to turn ourselves in the right direction. We want to be set straight and given the power to walk where we've been directed. Secondly, because we are who we are, we need to be given what can only be described as the personal ministry of God, in terms that we can understand, in physical and concrete form. We want this ministry to be as closely related to our human lives as Jesus' ministry was to the Jewish men and women who knew him.

Many people, reading the Biblical accounts, are so struck by what happened on Pentecost that they neglect to ask what happened the day after, and the day after that, and all the succeeding days. Having been invaded (as it were) by the Holy Spirit, what did the apostles and disciples do afterward? We can sense something of what they felt—the awe and wonder, and the joy and assurance given by the Spirit. But for us it is more important that we find out what came next. We weren't there ourselves, so we need to know what connection there is between that glory and our dreams of peace.

What the apostles did was to carry on the ministry of Jesus. They preached, of course, but they did much more. As Jesus had told them to do, they baptized. They also gathered together to give thanks and to participate in the Lord's Supper, as He had commanded them to do. These were two specific things they had been commissioned for. Furthermore, they continued doing what Jesus had done. They healed the sick. They forgave the sins of the sick at heart. And they sent others out to do the same.

From one perspective, it sometimes looks as if the apostles and disciples took an exalted view of their own position in the world. Accepting Jesus' ministry is one thing. Accepting the ministry of the apostles—accepting the Church, in fact—is for some people quite another matter. Hence the occasional assertion that "I'm a Christian, but I don't believe in the organized Church," as if Christianity were a state of mind or a sentiment.

In point of fact, the apostles and disciples and their descendants gave to the world, and still give, something a great deal more important than any organizational form could possibly contain. The Holy Spirit lives and moves within the Church to do what Jesus did, even now, twenty centuries after Pentecost. The Church offers—to anyone who asks—the power of God embodied in events and decisions of daily life. This power, usually referred to as *grace*, is not dispensed as if it "belonged" to the Church, like money or buildings, because no one has an exclusive franchise on the love of God. Rather, the Church acts as a conduit. It ministers to men and women as Jesus did, using the same basic elements of human existence that he used, to give human beings the power to live. Instead of denying the world, Jesus transformed it. He took the most ordinary of things, filled them with his own power, and returned them to his followers.

The physical, personal ministrations of God extended to us by the Church are called *sacraments*—in the traditional definition, "outward and visible signs of inward and spiritual grace." The power we cannot manufacture ourselves, then, is given through quite simple things and events. We do not necessarily perceive that power instantaneously, as the Apostles perceived the Holy Spirit at Pentecost. But we can grasp the exterior signs of power, and we certainly can see its effects in our lives.

We organize our human situations by means of many gods, even when we are trying very hard not to, and because we do, we are not unacquainted with the sacramental principle. All actions or things which communicate to us, in some concrete way, the power of our lesser saviors are "sacramental." A Thanksgiving dinner, for instance, with all the children and grandchildren and aunts and uncles gathered around the table, communicates the power and strength of "family." By reuniting people who have been separated, it enables us to set aside petty squabbles and to rediscover our common heritage. (Of course, it may sometimes communicate a less attractive power.) The loving hug a parent gives a baby communicates a kind of strength that cannot fully be understood by the baby, that still assists the baby to grow up with emotional serenity. A handshake, a Christmas present, a goodnight kiss—all sorts of things transmit a sort of "grace" that touches and empowers us, however briefly. These lesser sacramental events reflect the process of the Church's sacraments, except, of course, that they are human and therefore inevitably flawed.

The particular sacraments that carry within them the power of God have the same concrete and human characteristics that we associate with Jesus' ministry, although the forms they have taken historically and the attitudes with which Christians have approached them have been subject to a good deal of argument and controversy. The Church is, after all, made up of human beings, even as it is ultimately directed by the Holy Spirit. Rites have come and gone, labelled as sacraments in one generation, fallen into disuse in another. In the Middle Ages, for example, exorcism (casting out of devils) was regarded as a sacrament. It fell into disuse when anxiety about devils ceased to be an important element in Christian thought. While a lot of people have re-discovered the rite in recent years, it still has not been re-elevated to the status of a sacrament.

Some Christians, looking to Jesus' specific commandments, accept only Baptism and Holy Communion as sacraments, since these were ordained by him. Others would add to the list the actions Jesus performed—healing of the sick, forgiving sins, and so on. Because it is the Church which gives form to the sacraments, differences among Christian groups have contributed to the problem, as have historical clashes over meanings to be attached to the sacramental principle. Does the "outward and visible sign" somehow change in character when it becomes the vehicle for God's power? When we are baptized with water, do we have to be immersed, or may water be poured on the head? From one point of view, some of the questions about sacraments seem faintly foolish, but the questions themselves bear witness to the seriousness with which Christians take the power of sacraments.

Of the sacraments that have lasted out the various changes in culture and civilization, only two are generally agreed upon among all Christians today: Baptism and Holy Communion. These are described in the Episcopal Prayer Book as "generally necessary," because they are available to all and because they were ordained by Jesus.

Despite differences of opinion and tradition and variations in emphasis, the sacramental way remains the same. We turn away from our lesser saviors and their ways to the Church— the people of God. In so doing, we give our disordered lives to God and are united with Him. Then we are given our lives back, filled with the power of God. Ordinary physical events— things and actions belonging to the world in which we live— become the vehicles of God's love and power, conveying to us the strength to live both in the world and in God's Kingdom. It is not required that we make ourselves over. It is not even required that we make over everything around us. It is only required that we accept the gifts given to us, although, oddly enough, some of us find the act of acceptance to be more difficult than we might have thought. Still the Christian sacraments are far more powerful than we are. God ministers to us in physical, tangible ways in the context of the very world that so often defeats and wounds us.

Baptism is the starting point. It is the sacrament of rebirth, recreation. By symbolically washing us, the Church turns us around and sets us straight. The Book of Common Prayer describes this process by various analogies: the means by which God "adopts us as his children," "union with Christ in his death and resurrection," "new life in the Holy Spirit." In Baptism, we are made part of the Church, taken into the Body of Christ. However the sacrament is defined or described, its primary effect is an alteration in the direction of our lives, as we are given the power to live within the Kingdom.

The relationship with God that is established in Baptism is like a new birth because we are made into His children, and it is no accident that references to childhood are so prominent in the baptismal service. The human condition of sin is not something that we suffer from only after we have grown up. We are plagued by it simply by being born human. To be whole and well, we really need to start over, to allow ourselves to be "children" again, so that we can grow up again, only now in the way God directs us.

To be sure, the new relationship with God may not necessarily be worked out in practice. Plenty of baptized people show little sign of anything like a rebirth, or, if they do, it seems short-lived. But we must make the distinction between what is made available to us and what we do about it. When we turn away from our old lives and are given a new start, the union with God has been established, whether it bears fruit or not. When we are initiated into the community of God's people, into this new family, we may or may not take full advantage of its nurture, for at no point in our journey does God strip us of our freedom of choice.

Since this new relationship to God and His people constitutes the fundamental point of Baptism, Christians make a radical distinction between those who have been baptized and those who have not. Needless to say, we can get into any number of arguments about what happens to the unbaptized after death, and so on, but the arguments really get us nowhere because they usually start from the mistaken assumption that Baptism is what gets people into a heaven that begins when life ends. On the contrary, unless we are started out all over again, we cannot hope for much change in our lives here and now, and the Kingdom of Heaven referred to by Jesus is a lot more than life after death. Baptism is for a new life now, for becoming part of the Kingdom in the midst of our present existence.

> " 'Truly, truly, I say to you, unless one is born anew, he cannot see the kingdom of God .... unless one is born of water and the Spirit, he cannot enter into the kingdom of God. That which is born of the flesh is flesh, and that which is born of the Spirit is spirit. Do not marvel that I said to you, "You must be born anew." ' " (John 3: 3–7)

When Jesus talked this way, he was describing the way things are. He was not outlining the admissions requirement to a sort of celestial club. We need to be different people, and Baptism is the way this need is fulfilled, not by our efforts, but by God's grace.

Confirmation ratifies Baptism, completing the process begun with the pouring on of water. While in Baptism the new Christian has been started over and has been incorporated into the Church, in Confirmation the Holy Spirit empowers him or her to live a grown-up Christian life. In the early Church, as well as in the Orthodox Churches today, Confirmation and Baptism were one rite. Within the Western Churches, however, the two became separated and now are administered at different points in life. Since Baptism is so frequently administered to babies or small children, Confirmation has taken on the quality of a decision to be made, the choice to ratify an earlier Baptism. In this sense, it requires some degree of mature understanding of what Christianity is all about. Whether Confirmation is regarded as a separate sacrament, as the completion of Baptism, or as a sacramental rite, it affords to us the strengthening power of the Holy Spirit for living a new life:

> "Strengthen, O Lord, your servant ... with your Holy Spirit; empower *him* for your service; and sustain *him* all the days of *his* life ..."

With this prayer and the laying on of hands, the Bishop "confirms"—in the sense of "making strong" but also in the sense of "validating"—the rebirth originally given in Baptism. So when we look at the two rites together, we perceive how the Church answers our demand for a means by which we can be saved from ourselves. The water of Baptism and the laying on of hands in Confirmation are ordinary bits of life, set aside and made particular channels of God's power. Having been reborn, turned around, and set straight, we are also given the ability to walk in our new direction, however awkward and unsteady our steps.

Holy Communion is the other sacrament specifically ordained by Jesus. Its prototype is the meal we have come to call the Last Supper, the final meal of Christ and his Apostles on the night before his death. That supper was a Passover gathering, the same sort of gathering that still takes place in Jewish homes today. But there was one substantial difference. Jesus turned the occasion into something more than a *seder* by giving the Apostles bread and wine that he identified as his Body and Blood, and by telling them to "do this for the remembrance of me." Christians repeat his actions sacramentally.

In the Holy Communion, God renews—week by week and day by day—the relationship to Him and to each other already established in Baptism. He feeds the reborn with the only kind of food that satisfies our real needs. The Communion is offered to us all our lives long. Yet it is always new, as each moment for which we need strength is a new moment. Furthermore, the strength we get from this sacrament is not simply individual or personal. The language of the rite, for instance, is noticeably plural. It is "we," not "I," who give thanks. It is "we" who pray to be "made one body with Him, that He may dwell in us, and we in Him." Holy Communion is more than a private source of power; it is at once an activity of the Church and the lifegiving sustenance which knits it together.

The form this sacrament takes speaks to our longing for something more than words to help us, as we struggle to perceive our role in the Kingdom. No one assumes more than a beginning and a ratification of that beginning in Baptism and Confirmation. We are still going to find the going difficult. We will find ourselves tending to fall away, back into our old patterns, back to the familiar human situation. Just as a newborn baby needs to be fed if it is to live, so we need food (of a different sort, to be sure) to keep on living our new life. The food must, of course, be food with more than ordinary qualities. Parish suppers, for instance, provide physical nourishment as well as the much-needed opportunity for Christians to meet and talk together and enjoy a sense of belonging. But for the daily crises of human existence, only Holy Communion provides Christ's living food.

Bread and wine are "made holy" in the rite, are changed into sacramental nourishment by Christ's presence. When the Church talks about Christ's presence in the Communion, we may feel uneasy. It seems a very commonplace thing for Christ to be doing, especially when we start thinking about the worthiness of those who are being given this sacrament. Few, if any, of us can claim to deserve to share physically in Christ's life. Yet we all must live by some power. If we shy away from the power of Christ in the sacrament he ordained, by what power are we to live? Without the sacrament of Holy Communion we will almost surely tend to return to the lesser "sacraments" we have wished to put aside. The ritual of the dinner table, the tradition of "happy hour," the communion of the coffee break—we will be looking for strength in these. The strength we find may or may not prove sufficient. It will not sustain us for life.

As to the question of deserving to participate in Christ's feast, our worthiness has no bearing. The Holy Communion is the bread and wine of a whole new life, not a prize for good behavior. It is given to us because we cannot live in the Kingdom without it. It is not earned. "For my flesh is food indeed, and my blood is drink indeed. He who eats my flesh and drinks by blood abides in me, and I in him." (John 6:55–56)

Besides the two "necessary" sacraments, as well as Confirmation, there are other rites that can give sacramental help to us on our journey. These are regarded as sacraments in some Christian communities. Others define them as "services," still others as sacramental rites. They are not ordained by Christ in the specific manner of Baptism and Holy Communion, but they have withstood the test of history and remain of significant importance in the life of Christians. Two of them are designed for the purpose of enabling us to live particular kinds of life within the Christian Church. Two others are for moments of crisis.

Holy Matrimony is a lot more than the sentimental dressing-up of civil marriage. It provides God's power for one of the most demanding of human relationships. Because living together in such a manner as to allow for both individual growth and shared responsibility requires more than romantic love and good intentions, the Church provides the strength of God in Holy Matrimony. Men and women frequently start out in marriage with the assumption that merely making a commitment will somehow ensure a successful relationship, only to find that events and circumstances alter people, that people change, that the best of relationships are maintained only at a very real and frequently burdensome cost. Furthermore, to live as a Christian within marriage places extra demands on men and women. We have been told that Christ lives in his people, but it is frequently difficult to see Christ in the context of arguments over money, uncapped toothpaste tubes, sex, and unwashed dishes. Hence the need for *Holy* Matrimony, as opposed, perhaps, to a wedding that takes place in a church.

Christian marriage is a way of life within the wider way of Christianity. In sacramental marriage, the Church extends God's love, forgiveness, and power to the happy couple, so that, as the years go by, they can do more than simply tolerate each other. Obviously, not everyone chooses marriage as a way of life. Equally, not everyone ought to. Hence, Holy Matrimony is said not to be "necessary for salvation." But it *is* available. This bit of life is as much a vehicle for God's grace as is the fellowship of the Church.

Whenever the subject of Christian marriage comes up, so does the subject of divorce and remarriage after divorce. Enough has been said on this question that we are fully aware of the disapproval (to put it mildly) with which the Church views a break in the relationship. Sometimes it appears that the Church is insensitive to marital problems, as it seems insensitive to other human tragedies. But there is a valid reason for the general Christian concern that marriages endure. Holy Matrimony is God's gift, not something to be tried out and then discarded. In fact, it is given for life: "Those whom God has joined together let no one put asunder." So Christian marriage involves more than the decision of two people. God is part of the agreement.

People do, of course, enter into matrimony in such a way that there is no possibility of a sacramental union, in which case, the Church may declare the marriage "null"—that is, never to have been sacramental. And sometimes impediments show up after marriage that make the continuation of the relationship impossible. All too frequently, either the man or the woman or both have no real understanding of what Christian marriage is all about, so that what was intended to be sacramental is no such thing. Nonetheless, the union is an enduring one, endowed with God's power, so that, if we wish, we can live fruitfully in this world of marriage as well as in the Kingdom of God.

Holy Orders provide the same kind of sacramental help as Holy Matrimony, this time for the particular work of the ordained ministry. All Christians are ministers, to be sure, because all Christians are called to take care of other people, to pray, to serve God, and to help others to find Christ. But the clergy are called to do specific jobs within the Church, and the list of jobs they are required to perform demands more than a general willingness to conduct Church services or help people in trouble.

Clergy, of course, answer the same call heard by every Christian, but the ordained ministry has a specific function within the Church. Clergy administer the sacraments to those committed to their charge, and they preach and teach the Gospel. This seems straightforward enough. But as they live in terms of their commissions, they are called to be much more. They are pastors, administrators, office managers, public relations experts, teachers of all age levels, and sometimes janitors. They need, in turn, unwearying patience, ingenuity, stability, intellect, honesty, and a good measure of salesmanship. The expectations laid upon the clergy by their people and by their commitment to their calling frequently demand more of them than they can possibly fulfill—on their own. The sacramental rite of Holy Orders provides God's help, so that those who are ordained can fill the shoes they have agreed to wear.

A good many clergy seem to us to be deficient in the qualities and abilities we would like them to have. Most of us realize that deficiencies are inevitable. The clergy are human, as we all are, although we persist in thinking that those who are ordained have the obligation to be "professional" Christians, more skilled in the art of living in the Kingdom than we. In a way, however, even the clergy's failures only emphasize the need for God's power for this and every other vocation. Ordination communicates that power, as the Holy Communion renews it. But no one—not even the clergy—makes use of God's power at all times. Fortunately for all concerned, human weaknesses and problems do not negate God's power; they only hinder our own lives within the Kingdom.

Two other sacramental rites—*Holy Unction* and *Penance*—repair and restore those who are inhibited in the Christian life by physical sickness and habitual vice. Bodily illness has a way of dramatizing for us our human need for a savior. When we find ourselves having to cope with pain and death, we are at our most helpless, indeed at our most human. Someone has to save us, because we cannot save ourselves. Similarly, our vices have a nasty way of maintaining their stranglehold on our lives. We keep slipping back, despite our excellent intentions, and unless we are fortunate in our vices, we can easily wind up hating ourselves.

Unction, the anointing of the sick with oil, or the laying on of hands, is the sacramental rite of healing—healing not only of sick bodies, but of sick and fearful souls. In serious illness, we experience all at once the devastation of human sin—pain, fear, worry, extreme loneliness, anger, even terror. We look straight into the unknown. Other people may sympathize with us, but they cannot share our pain, because pain has isolated us from everyone around us. Naturally we call in specialists, nurses, therapists, in search of relief; but all too often the experts cannot really make us well. So, if we have responded to the call of Christ, we turn to God for the strength to be sick in a way that will let us perceive the Kingdom even in our helplessness.

For some, Unction means physical and spiritual healing, a means to "release you from suffering, and restore you to wholeness and strength." The gift of power for illness may mean the renewal of the body; certainly it means the renewal of our capacity to live as Christians with the strain of illness. For others, the rite helps in the crossing of death's irrational barrier. Indeed, for many centuries Unction was known as the Last Rites and was considered a sign that death was imminent. In more recent years, with the upsurge of interest in spiritual healing, the rite has been put into sacramental place as healing. In whichever light it is seen, the power of God is not limited by the progress of the illness. Rather, the experiences of sickness and death are made as much a part of Christian living as are health and life.

Penance is sacramental confession. It is all too frequently misunderstood. It is neither an easy way out of a bad jam or a quick fix for a painful conscience, nor is it a convenient license to commit as many vices as we like. Whether we intend it or not, when we lapse from our God-given state of union with

Him and each other—even though the lapse may be only momentary—our vices come galloping back. We start exhibiting all the same old symptoms: losing tempers or sulking; yearning after money, or whatever. Penance provides the means by which God's forgiveness is sacramentally given us. As Baptism deals with original sin, so Penance deals with our post-Baptismal bad behavior.

"By his authority committed to me, I absolve you from all your sins. . . ." With these words, the priest, acting as a representative of the Church, absolves the penitent from guilt. Confession to the Church in the person of the priest is not an easy way of dealing with habitual vices, but for many Christians it has proven invaluable. It is not obligatory—nothing with sacramental character can be forced on people, and no Christian is ever coerced into receiving God's grace. Penance is a gift for those who need and wish it.

Our attitudes toward the whole idea of sacraments as God's personal touch in our lives, as the means whereby we enter and live within His Kingdom, are conditioned by many factors. For instance, if we are still committed to the proposition that the Church ought to be chiefly concerned with giving good advice or providing moral guidance, then the sacramental way will have little meaning for us. Some of us still may be suffering from the widespread conviction that there is something basically anti-spiritual about the material world. If so, then we simply cannot see how God could work through the physical channels of sacraments. Or perhaps we think that God and the Church only have to do with life after death. If so, we are likely to see little reason for sacraments, which are, after all, given for our daily lives. And of course, one of our most deeply felt reservations may come from the sense that the Church, source of the sacraments, is only a substitute for a personal and direct experience of God, a sort of second best for those of us born too late to know Jesus Christ.

Objections and reservations about the sacramental way cannot be satisfactorily met until we become fully and clearly aware of the extent to which we long for the Kingdom of God. Sacraments are answers to needs, and only as we have identified our helplessness, in whatever of the various forms it shows in our lives, will we perceive how the sacramental way turns out to be the road we are traveling on.

SIX

Prayer

Whatever our religious training and position has been, we are all likely to agree at least on the importance of prayer, probably because we all pray, even if not to a traditional God. There is no organized religion which does not regard prayer as one of the fundamental activities of human life, and there is no time in life when prayer is not appropriate. It is a comfort to the little child who can say "our Father, who art in heaven . . . ." and climb into bed feeling warm and secure. It is a source of strength for the sick, who find reassurance in the familiar words of assurance and dependence. It is a refuge for us when we are desperate, when every other course has failed. We may not be able to do anything about a given predicament, but we can always pray.

There are difficulties with prayer, too. Sometimes we find ourselves praying out of anger and frustration. There are frequent times when we don't know to whom we are praying, when the words seem to be cast into an unanswering void. For some, prayer is a chore. It does not seem to come naturally, but must be worked at and practiced. For others, prayer may bring on a sense of guilt. Aware as we are that we only pray when we're in trouble, we are afraid to pray lest we be hypocritical.

Prayer is one of the most intimate of human activities. We pray in such personal terms that, even though we know everybody else prays, we find vocal prayers awkward, even embarrassing, when said out loud in public (except by preachers, who get paid to do so). In one sense, prayer always expresses our relationships to God, and because our relationships vary according to our situations, so do our prayers vary. Furthermore, since these relationships are not static, our prayers change. This variability accounts for the fact that books about prayer may or may not be helpful. But the intimacy of prayer creates its own problems. Some of us cannot quite see how an activity so personal and individual can be successfully translated into a group experience. Thus the custom of saying grace before meals can prove uncomfortable unless we grow up with it. Corporate prayer, as in a Church service, may seem downright strange, unless we learned to pray within the Church.

Prayer is a two-way process. It is communication between God as Himself and human beings as themselves. As such, it always includes more than the forms that we use. For example, there are times when our sense of gratitude to God—for a narrow escape, for a joyful event, for sudden relief from pain—is so all-inclusive that we really don't say a word but are thankful all over. On the other hand, there are times when no matter how hard we try to be polite to God, the angry "Why me, O God?" saturates the words we recite. And there are occasions in which we find ourselves really praying to ourselves, not God. Our formal expressions of thanks really express self-satisfaction: "Thank God I'm better than they are."

In the Kingdom of God, of course, prayer is not the only way of knowing God, or reaching out to Him, because communication with God is never limited by words or attitudes or actions.

The Church, as God's community, and the sacraments, as the channels of God's power, are other ways of knowing Him and allowing Him to reach us. These encounters with God are, in terms of our understanding, indirect. God cloaks Himself, as it were, under the guise of familiar relationships, things, words, and actions. Prayer is encounter with different terms.

It is direct, immediate, not requiring human relationships, things, words, or actions. An analogy to the distinction between these forms of encounter—the direct and the indirect—might be found in the marriage relationship. A husband and wife do a lot of communicating in words and action. Yet as they live their lives out together, there will be many times when they communicate with each other without words.

It is the indirectness of the encounter with God in Church and sacrament that sometimes leads us to feel that prayer is the "better" channel of communication. Although God may be calling to us through any number of indirect means—an appeal for famine relief, the needs of a sick or bereaved neighbor, a sermon in Church, or the Christian Education Committee's appeal for teachers—we fail to hear and respond because we can't perceive Him directly. The notion that we encounter God in the Church as well as in prayer is one we often overlook, if not reject. The same misunderstanding occurs in our attitudes toward the sacraments. If there were some way in which God spoke to us directly at the turning points in our lives, we might be more willing to hear Him. But He is hidden. No voice from a cloud pronounces the absolution of sin. Confirmation is not marked by tongues of fire. The bread and wine of Communion look and taste exactly like bread and wine. Meanwhile, private prayer is often marked by lovely feelings, by emotions, by "spiritual" sensations. According to our common tendency to exalt that which is not of this world, then, we assume that prayer is the "higher" communion.

Yet if prayer is so much more direct (or uncluttered or unfettered or however we wish to put it), why is it so hard for some of us to pray? Why does prayer sometimes seem more like practicing scales on the piano than like playing a concerto?

The chief barrier to our life of prayer is our lack of experience of God. Unless and until we have identified His power in our lives, we cannot be sure who we are or who He is, what we are doing as we pray, and how He is responding to us. As any two people must learn each other's ways through words and actions before there can be any direct encounter between them, so we cannot be wholly at ease with God in prayer until we have experienced Him in Church and sacrament. This is not to say that we cannot pray until we know all about God. We always pray, sometimes to Him (even when we have no idea who He is) and even more frequently to whatever and whoever our human saviors are. It is our sense of *ease* in prayer that depends on experience. It is no accident that we beg, implore, petition, adore, only those human saviors whom we know to be real powers in our lives. The same requirement obtains in our relationships with God. Until we know Him to be the real power in our lives, we will feel some constraint in praying to Him.

For many of us, then, prayer can be a hard job because the other Person with whom we are trying to communicate is sometimes incomprehensible. It is difficult to understand Him. As children we probably prayed for something we did not get. It seems silly now, looking back, but the fact that we did not get a new bike for Christmas may have led us to decide that God has a mean streak. From the adult standpoint, there is nothing mysterious about what happened then. We were probably much too young for a two-wheeler, or else there simply was no money for bikes. Yet the same experience keeps on happening to us as adults. One moment God "answers" our prayers, which makes us feel wonderful; the next moment He seems to ignore us. Sometimes He heals the sick, sometimes He doesn't, and we are left wondering what we did wrong. Sometimes He saves us from the consequences of our actions, sometimes He doesn't, and we don't see the difference.

Perhaps we are so limited by our moods and feelings that we cannot make ourselves stick to prayer for more than a minute or two at a time, a common situation that happens both when we are alone and when we are saying prayers in Church. Just when we ought to be face-to-face, so to speak, with the God who made us, our minds begin to wander. We find ourselves thinking about what to have for lunch instead of about God's mercy. We hash over an upcoming job interview instead of the General Confession. Or we find ourselves sayings things we don't mean. We say "Thank you, Lord" and don't feel a thing. We confess we have sinned and feel no sense of repentance at all.

So prayer—direct and immediate as it is—is not without its problems and is not always more meaningful to us than are the sacraments and the Church. Encounters with God are, in some ways, not much different from encounters with other people. We learn about people first by what they do and how they behave. Only then can we begin to trust them, to rely on them, to understand how they matter to us. So it is with God. We are not born into a natural relationship with Him. On the contrary, we know very little about Him until His love and power are made known to us in His actions. Because we can neither see nor hear Him, we observe His love in hidden ways. We can only put our faith in Him as He makes His power known to us in our personal histories.

There are five kinds of prayer: petition, intercession, confession, thanksgiving, and adoration.

Petition is just what it sounds like: asking for things or benefits for ourselves. Naturally, this seems self-centered. We always seem to be asking God for something, like spoiled children who never know when to quit saying "Gimme." To be sure, the Gospel quotes Jesus as saying "Ask, and it will be given you; seek, and you will find; knock, and it will be opened to you." (Luke 11:9) Yet when it comes down to the asking, we feel like hypocrites. How do we dare ask for things, when we spend so little of our attention on God? The analogy of children and parents makes our consciences smart. We know what we think of children whose demands for attention are not matched by attentive care for their parents.

But Jesus meant what he said. There is little point in being high-minded about petitionary prayer, when God knows perfectly well what is in our hearts. He is not like earthly parents, who are as much in need of love as their children are. On the contrary, petitionary prayer, however self-centered it seems, reinforces our sense of who we are and who God is. It is a means of admitting our own ability to be in charge of ourselves.

It is also an admission—to ourselves—that the question of "deserving" God's love and power simply does not apply. If we are to be honest with ourselves (and with God) it is better not to pretend that we *can* make ourselves good enough to ask Him for what we want, even "our daily bread."

It ought to go without saying that we do not always need the things we are praying for, but somehow this obvious fact frequently escapes our notice. The four-year-old does not really need a chemistry set, and we do not necessarily need a new job or a new mate. Indeed, even our most desperate petitions may be rooted in our incapacity to perceive what is truly important in our lives. Suppose we plead for freedom from pain and get no immediate relief. The pain we are asking to be free from may be doing us a life-giving service, by functioning as a symptom of a fatal disease. We, in our ignorance, get angry at God for "not hearing," while failing to appreciate the fact that petition is not the same thing as an aspirin tablet. Our inability to know what we need is why the answer to a petition is often "No," or "Not now." It is also why we usually qualify our petitions with the words "Thy will be done."

We may wonder if there is any use in petitionary prayer, since God is the only judge of what is good for us, if our petitions seem always to be answered in the negative. Actually, the eternal value of petition is to be found in the relationship out of which it emerges. We are praying out of the conviction that it is God who saves us and God who gives us the power to live. We are also praying out of the conviction that God loves us, selfish as we are. Petition has been described as daring to be real with God, to be free to say, "I can't help wanting these things I ask for, but You know me. I trust You enough to say I want this, and I leave it in Your hands to judge the wisdom of my having it."

Intercession turns other people over to God's care. We substitute ourselves, our relationship with God, for someone who has a particular need of God's power, for someone who (either because of his or her own barrier of sin or because of circumstances) is unable or unwilling to pray, or for those we love, whom we simply want to place in God's hands. The notion of substitution—that X can pray on behalf of Y—is one of the great characteristics of God's Kingdom. It grows out of the fact that Christ died on our behalf, as a substitute for us all. He did for us what we couldn't do for ourselves. Intercession imitates his example: "Father, forgive them; for they know not what they do." (Luke 23:34)

Does intercession do any good? The same factors apply here that apply to petitionary prayer. Actually, we may have no idea at all what another person really needs. Perhaps we are praying for someone's recovery from illness. We may know very little about the relationship between that person and God, and that relationship may be deepening because of the illness. Misconceptions and prejudices may be melting away. Trust may be gradually replacing anger. Pain may be altering thoughtlessness into concern for others. The importance of intercession is not found in God's answer to the prayer. Rather, it is found in the twofold relationship it expresses: the love of God and the love of other human beings.

Confession is not at all the same thing as self-abasement or grovelling. It is the objective admission to God of our transgressions and of our predicament. Since we do not as a rule like to think about our transgressions in their entirety, we are inclined to concentrate our confessions to God around the ones that are socially embarrassing or generally inconvenient. Confession goes much deeper than this. It is the whole human being who meets God in prayer. We cannot leave behind, tucked away out of sight like a skeleton in the closet, the parts of our lives that we don't like to think about. So self-examination—the open-eyed scrutiny of our daily lives—precedes confession. It helps us to see ourselves as we are.

Confession, we can remind ourselves, is the second step of a process already begun in Baptism. We have already been forgiven by God for the sin that set us apart from Him. Thus confession is not something we have to do in order to earn forgiveness. Rather, it is the kind of prayer that widens and deepens our knowledge of ourselves, a form of communication that allows us to be ourselves, our total selves, before God.

Confession is also the means by which we accept God's forgiveness. In a very real sense, it is among the most important forms of prayer, for God's forgiveness needs getting used to. We are accustomed to looking at forgiveness as a sort of benevolent overlooking of our offenses, as if they didn't really matter or weren't really our fault. But forgiveness includes the recognition of an offense. In other words, it includes judgment. When we forgive each other, we are at the same time judging each other. This is sometimes a very painful process, as we very well know, the more painful if we disagree with the judgment. God's forgiveness, too, involves judgment. But the problem with His forgiveness is that unless we have recognized our offenses, His judgment is likely to be considerably more far-reaching than anything we bargained for. So we face the forgiveness of God with the prayer of confession, which helps us to understand more and more clearly the nature of our sin and the pervasiveness of our behavior patterns. It also helps us to accept the element of judgment in God's forgiveness, to accept His forgiveness for the things we didn't know we did, as willingly as we accept the same forgiveness for the awful things we know we've done. Unless confession is familiar territory for us, God's forgiveness is bound to come as something of a shock.

Thanksgiving is the declaration of our gratitude and our indebtedness to God. It takes a good may forms, from the relieved "Thank God!" we feel when IRS sends a refund to the deep sense of inexpressible gratitude that follows deliverance from some dreadful calamity. Sometimes, thanksgiving comes naturally and easily. Our lives are filled with so many blessings that we really do *want* to give thanks. Indeed, the more we pray in thanksgiving, the more blessings we can count, and thanksgiving can become so interwoven into the fabric of life that almost all our praying is marked by it.

But there are times when we cannot find much to be thankful about. And there are times when thanksgiving seems virtually impossible, as when someone dear to us dies. It is at this point in life when the daily experience in giving thanks pays off. We usually start out thanking God only for those things and events that we like. This habit begins to spread into other, deeper occasions for thanks, as we begin to catch sight of the good in things and events that we at first thought painful. We can be thankful, for instance, that we didn't get promoted or didn't get married. As this kind of insight into thanksgiving develops, it becomes easier to give thanks under what are (to others) unlikely circumstances. The promise of Christianity is that we may be free not only to bear all kinds of impossible burdens, but even to learn the art of thankfulness under them. No one—not even a devout Christian—is pretending that the world is perfect, or that there is not pain in our existence. Yet in the Good News of Christ is the hint that there is some use for pain and some sense in the events which transpire in our lives. Jesus said, " 'I am the true vine, and my Father is the vinedresser . . . every branch that does bear fruit he prunes, that it may bear more fruit.' " (John 15:1–2) Our response to Christ's call enables us to see the fruit and to give thanks both for it and for the pruning.

It should be emphasized that this is not a Pollyanna sort of praying. We have to admit to ourselves and to God that we do not enjoy what is happening to us. It takes some time, for instance, to perceive that our pain has resulted in more and better fruit. The key to thanksgiving is not to be found in our feelings, but in the perspective we have of what happens to us. Christian thanksgiving enables us to see both pains and "blessings" in a new fashion, because thanksgiving, like confession, is a way of revealing us to ourselves, We are beginning to look at the good things in life as deriving not from our own efforts, but from God.

This kind of praying acts as a checkrein on our arrogance. It delivers us from the compulsion to measure all things by their effects on our personal comfort. It also delivers us from the compulsion to pat ourselves on the back. Thanksgiving, then, becomes an increasingly fertile ground of communication with the Lord of life. It is no accident that the rite of Holy

Communion is so frequently called the Holy Eucharist, since the greek word *"evcharistó"* means "thank you."

Adoration is, as the Book of Common Prayer puts it, "the lifting up of the heart and mind to God, asking nothing but to enjoy God's presence." (p. 857) In one sense, adoration quite simply means the enjoyment of our relationship with God. Since we spend a lot of our time praying that the relationship be made more comfortable than it is, we sometimes are not aware that there are moments when we are simply basking in the knowledge that we don't have to be in charge, that we don't have to be remorseful, that we don't have to ask unanswerable questions, that we just can be ourselves and be glad that God is Himself.

To be sure, any time we pray, we are implicitly renouncing our claim to independence. If we knew we could manage by ourselves, we wouldn't be praying. The problem is that we frequently are driven to acknowledge a helplessness that we either do not really feel or that we resent. At such times, prayers of adoration, with all that they imply, seem excessive or overstated.

But finding ourselves increasingly comfortable in our relationship with God opens endless possibilities within adoration, so that what might have seemed excessive turns out to be increasingly expressive of what we really know to be true. Such classic prayers of adoration as "Holy, holy, holy Lord, God of power and might . . ." and "Glory to God in the highest, and peace to his people on earth . . ." become personal as well as corporate hymns, packed with individual meanings.

For most of us, when prayer is experienced at its high points, the act of praying is intensely rewarding. Consequently, we are likely to be upset when it proves difficult or unrewarding. If God is always there and always God, and if we are here and always ourselves, then it seems bewildering that prayer can be such an uncertain encounter.

Yet any relationship undergoes change, if only because personalities change and develop. God is, of course, beyond change. But we are not. Because we do grow, suffer relapses, then grow in a new direction, prayer and the ways in which we pray are subject to many variations. Here again, however, experience comes to our aid. The changes in our life of prayer seem to fall into a fairly consistent pattern. This pattern is not a series of ever-higher steps for us to negotiate; it is more like a cycle, repeated over and over again in different contexts.

First, there are the subjective moments of prayer in which the experience seems altogether enlightening. These are wonder-filled moments. We are discovering God and our own helplessness. We are becoming acutely aware of our own creatureliness, but it does not offend us; on the contrary, we are relieved, full of gratitude, happy to let go. Our sensations are easily and painlessly expressed. The circumstances around us may vary widely, depending on what led to our new awarenesses. A conference, a church service, the conversation of a friend, a quiet moment alone—wherever it happens, we are suddenly aware of God's goodness, of His love. We have a strong sense of our own incapacity to earn that love, but we feel His presence so acutely that we find ourselves praying effortlessly and fluently.

The second stage in this cycle carries with it a certain measure of determination, along with resolutions to "do better from now on." We are trying to live up to the heights of the first stage, and so we try to behave in ways that are consistent with the way we felt then. But we discover that our attempts to live up to that stage cost us something. God is perfect and we are not. We discover the difference with real force when we enter the second stage of prayer. We're back at work again, the bills have to be paid. The arthritis hurts worse than ever, and the surroundings that were so conducive to prayer have slipped into the background. We can still remember the high point, but we don't seem to be able to capture it, let alone stay in it. As long as we retain something of the emotional flavor of the first stage, we pray fairly regularly and without too much difficulty. But our determination to pray tends to fade, along with the freshness of self-discovery. A period of what might be called neutrality ensues. We go on praying, out of the memory we have of what prayer could be, yet the "first fine careless rapture" is gone.

The third stage is sometimes called "spiritual dryness." This is the point at which we are likely to give up. Prayer made under this inhibiting dryness is still an encounter with God, but all the trimmings are missing. We have no sense of God's presence at all. The memory of the first stage now seems so faint as to be unreal. In fact, we feel quite "normal" once again. The Church and the sacraments carry us through spiritual dryness. When all we can manage are empty phrases and meaningless words, other people pray on our behalf. When we have no sense at all of God's presence, He is all around us, in the Holy Communion, in His people, in the events of our lives. For Christians this part of the cycle is made easier by the testimony of others who have themselves moved through and out of the arid stage into a different place. However difficult prayer is during these times, we are given assurance that spiritual dryness is not a permanent state of affairs.

Then, within a few days or a few months (cases lasting years have been known) the pattern repeats itself. God renews the process with another revelation of Himself, we discover ourselves once again, and we go through the same cycle. The difference is that each repetition of the cycle occurs on what might be called a more mature level. These successive stages may repeat themselves in varying degrees of intensity throughout life. However, as God leads us deeper and deeper into the life of the Kingdom, we are less and less dependent on emotional trimmings, and we attach less and less importance to sensations. Prayer is never easy, except at the high points, but it does become familiar territory. We gradually become capable of an honest expression of ourselves, just as we become more aware of God in our lives.

There are two general methods of praying, and both are used by Christians. *Personal* prayer is individual prayer, the expression to God of our individual needs, thanks, sorrows, and loves. This is our private prayer, but it is solitary rather than isolated, because we are still part of the Body of Christ, even as we pray by ourselves. It can be brief—just a phrase or two—or it can be fairly lengthy, if we find ourselves meditating. It can be vocal (although most of us like to be sure we are not overheard) or it can be silent. It can be routine, as in "Now I lay me down to sleep" or it can be free-ranging.

Personal prayer is more popular than *corporate* prayer—that is, group or common prayer. Yet Christians inevitably pray together. Personal prayer is given stability and direction by prayer undertaken with the community to which we belong. In common prayer we are praying as the Church. Our individual prayers are gathered, put in the plural, and summarized as common concerns. On the face of it, corporate prayer might seem to have only occasional pertinence to us as individuals with separate problems. But corporate prayer works because the concerns that evoke our individual prayers are, after all, only human concerns, which we share with everyone else.

Corporate prayer occasionally leads to hypocrisy. We find ourselves joining together in petitions for virtues we don't really want, or in the confession of vices we have no real intention of abandoning. On the other hand, personal prayer can lead us into religious isolationism, into excessive nurture of our own feelings, and even into a sort of "me and my God" perversion of Christianity. The Church calls us to make use of both methods. When we find ourselves slipping into one extreme, we are called back by the exercise of the other. Both methods are characteristic of God's Kingdom, yet neither is independent of the other.

Within these two methods there are two further categories of prayer. On the one hand, prayer may be *formal*, that is, fixed or ritual, as in the Book of Common Prayer. Or it may be *informal*, voiced in our own words and with or own variations. Many of us are brought up to believe that "book" prayers are somehow not as good as "made up" prayers. In fact, both are useful. Formal prayer teaches us to pray and helps us to an adult level of prayer. It also sustains us during spiritual dryness, when we can't think of anything to say to God. On the other hand, informal prayer can infuse new life into worship which has become so formal as to seem cut and dried.

Among the areas in which our lives seem to require help is this whole area of prayer. We would like to get specific answers to specific questions here, as well as in other problem spots. Should we pray at set times, say, morning and evening? Should we pray for things we don't really need, but would secretly like to have? Should we pray over every little decision we face, or should we reserve prayer for the major turning points? Should we pray for our enemies, even when they are wicked and godless? Should we pray when we are angry?

These questions, and the others like them, can be answered, of course. We pray all the time, not simply at set moments, although it helps us become experienced in prayer if we inject a little discipline into it. We pray for material things that we don't need, and we also pray that God's will be done with regard to them. We pray over minor decisions and over major ones. We pray for our enemies, because only God judges who is wicked and who is not. We pray when we're angry and when we're happy, when we are hurt and when we are not, when we are bitter and when we are forgiving.

But the questions themselves get answered only as we put behind us the notion of a standard by which we can measure our achievements in prayer. Encounters with God in prayer cannot be standardized. We can't work toward a minimum level with which to be content. Nor can we turn prayer into a sort of spiritual report card that tells us where we are on our journey.

What we do find is that prayer takes on new dimensions as we become more and more at ease with it. It deepens and spreads out until it becomes almost second nature to us. We learn to pray in more than words. Prayer goes on in our attitudes, our actions, our relationships with others. The types of prayer, the forms and methods we use, become relatively unimportant. And we even come to the point at which all questions about prayer seem irrelevant. This is the point at which the Kingdom of Heaven has become a living reality for us, even here, in the midst of the world in which we live.

SEVEN

God

Once we have begun to perceive the ways in which God works in our lives, we also begin to formulate what we know about Him. Actually, it is virtually impossible for us to say that we "know" Him, since He is, in terms of human definitions, beyond our knowing. In this regard, we are dependent entirely on His will. Either He allows us to see some aspect of His being, or He does not. And we are not the most reliable of witnesses, given the fact that we, for the most part, see God primarily as someone dedicated to fulfilling our needs, rather than as Himself alone.

An analogy might help us understand our situation. The family cat perceives human beings as providers of food and shelter, and sometimes affection. The cat knows nothing of our thoughts or emotions. It does not know what we do for a living or how much we value upholstered furniture. We are independent of, and different from, cats. God is independent of us. He is not simply a brand of medicine that will or will not cure our ailments. Consequently, while we are fond of debating about Him, our debates usually end up nowhere. He remains Himself, no matter what we say or think. However frequently our opinions change, and they do, He is beyond change. Anything—anyone—beyond change is beyond the realm of human reason and imagination, just as we are beyond the realm of cats.

Yet we remain curious about God, because we are struggling to form a religious relationship with Him. It is very much in our human nature to wish to know Him as well as we can. The curiosity we feel about God's person, His nature, and His activities, does not stem from total ignorance. On the contrary, most of us have been exposed from childhood on to an overabundance of opinions about Him. Arguments about His nature, for instance, sometimes turn out to be very public. If we were sent to church school as youngsters, we heard all sorts of stories about God's activities. If we had agnostics as teachers, we heard those same stories attacked. Somehow almost everyone has accumulated a collection of ill-digested information about God. How we sort it out and make sense of it depends almost entirely on the circumstances of our lives.

Unhappily, however, much of the information we have heard about God seems either irrelevant or contradictory. It really makes very little difference to most of us, for instance, whether or not God is a "Trinity." This is a speculative question, one to play with, but not one that has practical bearing on our individual problems. Again, we are not greatly disturbed by the notion that God is, as the Bible has it, a jealous God. Jealousy is a word we can understand only in human terms. We cannot quite take in the application of a human emotion to the idea of a God Who created the universe—a mind-boggling concept, given the incalculable size of the universe. Even the idea that God is intensely and intimately concerned with our daily lives is difficult to comprehend.

The irrelevance of many of our ideas about God shows up most clearly in conversations. Unless we have a friend whose troubles seem to require some reference to God, we usually find it downright embarrassing to talk about Him. Generally speaking, most of us simply do not think about Him often enough to know what to say. And even if we do think about Him, it is always risky to put our thoughts into words. It is as if He were everyone's possession, yet no one's. If, at a party, we make a statement about Him, the conversation either dies or else erupts into unpleasant arguments. For some people, God is like a cartoon clergyman—the original wet blanket. For the rest, He is a matter of opinion—and the louder the voice, the better the chance of winning the argument. Indeed, introducing God into a social occasion is tantamount to introducing a stranger about whom everyone has a story, but whom no one really knows.

More disturbing yet, many of our ideas about God are wildly at variance with each other. We can hardly avoid being uneasy, for example, when we are faced with the paradox of God's mercy and His justice. We are told that He is "slow to chide and swift to bless." Then we read the Bible and find a good deal of reference to the punishment of evildoers. On the other hand, all of us, it seems, will agree that He is righteous. We persist in saying this in the face of a great deal of untrammeled wickedness. We also hear much talk about God's loving power, yet we don't notice Him interfering when tragedies are in the making. Much is formally preached about God's omnipotence. But we act as if we had to defend Him and His goodness against other human beings. We never notice the irony: human beings trying to protect God from Communists and other unbelievers. We very rarely sort out and put in order our ideas about Him. If we did, we might find all kinds of inconsistencies. We might also find that we are incapable of reconciling our convictions.

Beneath these two problems—God's "irrelevance" and His "paradoxical" nature—is another, more personal problem. No matter how often and how eloquently we are told about Him, the information always seems to come to us secondhand. In reading the Bible, for instance, we are struck by the fact that the prophets and the psalmists can make statements about Him that we can neither refute with complete assurance nor adopt wholeheartedly. Both in the Old and the New Testaments, people are writing and talking about someone whom they have met and known more intimately than we. What they say about Him is probably more accurate than anything we could say, given the authoritative manner in which they speak. But we honestly do not know whether or not they are right. We do not much like the prophetic insistence that God can be angry at us. Yet how do we know whetner He is capable of anger, since we know so little about Him? On the other hand, we very much like to hear about His love. But how do we know whether He is capable of love?

We feel, much of the time, as if we are onlookers in this whole religious operation. We are trying to understand, but, as in some of the most highly recommended books, both the plot and the characters are over our heads. It might be that we could manage to get along contentedly enough, if only we were allowed to remain on the sidelines. Unfortunately, we ourselves are constantly being shoved into the action. We ourselves are characters who have the dim sense that the plot has meaning; yet someone forgot to tell us what we're supposed to do.

To take the literary analogy a little further, we find also that the Person who wrote the book, who seems to be directing the plot, and who is the chief character, is a stranger to us. All our knowledge about Him is derivative, coming to us from other characters, phrased in their language rather than ours, consisting of bits and pieces that we find often bewildering. We are not only confused as to what we ought to be saying and doing, but, as the plot moves along carrying us with it whether we understand it or not, we find we are afraid—afraid of God.

This combination of our sense of helplessness and all those secondhand bits of information about God brings us up against what is possibly the ultimate religious question: the problem of evil. Almost all religious thought begins here.

This is the problem: if the Being who is responsible for the universe is good, where did evil come from? Or, translated into more down-to-earth terms, if God is good, how can He permit things to be so bad?

Stated in this form, the problem of evil is merely a philosophical guessing game. It doesn't really matter in the least where evil came from, unless we happen to be playing around with general, philosophical terms, because evil, as an abstract, is of little importance to us—until it hits home. In other words, to argue about the problem of evil is interesting for some people; to experience the problem is devastating to anyone.

We have been told that God is loving and all-powerful. How, then, can He countenance what goes on daily in His world? A little child is brutally killed; a terrible forest fire wipes out an entire community; a flood devastates whole sections of a state; a loved parent, one who has always exemplified goodness, dies in agony from cancer. These things we recognize as evil, not some philosophical idea. This is what the problem of evil looks like to us.

But there is another side to the problem, one that can be called the problem of good. If this Being about whom we have been talking is really righteous, how in the world can He permit us to go on fouling His creation? Here we are, endowed with all kinds of potentialities for making the world good and beautiful and glorious. We have chosen to turn our backs on God, to kill and maim and hurt each other, to destroy the world around us wantonly, to live our lives in terms of greed and hatred, and in general to thumb our collective nose at the God who made us. We are like ants at a picnic, or termites. As human beings, we feel no remorse about killing obnoxious insects. Why does God refrain from destroying us? We may spend most of our time speculating about the problem of innocent suffering, but we rarely find time to puzzle over the problem of undeserved life.

Yet in both cases the basic premise is the same. God is presumed to be a certain Person with a known character that does not vary. But if He is what we think He is, and nothing greater, then something is wrong somewhere. He doesn't do what we expect Him to do.

The moment we find ourselves in an argument with an agnostic, our first line of fire is likely to be some such statement as: "If there is no God, how did the universe come into being"? We proceed, in other words, from the idea that our first tentative acquaintance with God stems from our inability to explain how all those innumerable galaxies came about. The only trouble with a personal theology that begins with the Creation is that this is not how our own religious experience begins.

Our first consciousness of a Being outside ourselves grows from the sense that we do not control our own lives. For infants and small children, the source of control is obviously their parents. But children grow up to become adults, and as adults we discover that being grown-up does not give us much more control over life than we had as babies. Things happen that are not within our understanding, and we develop the feeling that something larger than we are is interfering with human existence. So it is not the vastness and complexity of the universe that implies the existence of God. We don't spend much time mulling about such things. It is the uncontrollability of existence that we think about. We can neither halt nor explain much of what happens to us. At first we think it is "fate" or "providence" or spirits or gods that are shoving us around. Then, and only gradually, we perceive that there is some sort of pattern in what happens, that we are being pushed or pulled in certain directions, that the same things happen to other men and women. And out of our shared experience, we build myths and tragedies that describe the pattern.

As we notice the common direction in which we are being turned, and that we are all undergoing much the same experience, we find it unlikely that there could be a multitude of powers all engaged in doing the same thing, whether it be the downfall of the proud or the ridicule of the boastful. The parallels among human experiences point to parallels among human guesses about whatever controls us. Hence, the gods of one nation are similar to the gods of another, and spirit or fate or providence looks about the same to a Bantu as to an Eskimo. Or, on a more personal level, our own experience of whatever power shapes us corresponds to that of others, and if other people name this power God, then we too start talking about God.

It is from observation that we conclude that there is a Being—one Being, not many. This is a Being so much larger and more powerful than we that He controls all of life. We cannot understand His ways or His purposes, if any, but we can guess certain things about Him by the manner in which He treats us. For instance, from the fact that He seems to us to show attributes recognizable to us (even if not fully understood), we perceive in this Being some kind of personhood. We look at what happens and see an intelligence and coherence behind events, and we call this Being "He." In doing so, we ought not to be attributing gender to God, gender relating as it does to the physical body, and God clearly not so limited. Calling God "He" is only a way of attributing *personality* to this force that is greater than any we could possibly describe.

In time we find that this Person is far more deeply interested in us than we ourselves might have thought appropriate. Our first impressions are formed in terms of His power over us. But gradually we find that He is somehow involved in the way we live. If we pay attention to Him, it seems that we get along better than we do when we don't pay attention. It is as if He allows us to make agreements with Him. If we turn toward Him, worship Him, He makes it possible for us to live peacefully within the pressures of human existence.

Once we begin to pay attention to Him, we start discovering more and more about Him. He is not just larger than life-size, like a human being raised to the nth degree. He is of a different category altogether. At first we usually entertain the notion that He is pretty much like us, only unrestricted by death and physical limitations. We soon find out that it's the other way around. It is we who are a little like Him, only very restricted. He is righteous, for instance. That is, He is always *right*, always justified. We are sometimes right in what we think and do. Far more often, we are not.

Being the kind of creatures we are, we find this Person virtually incomprehensible. We cannot even talk about Him without committing the error of putting our own limitations on Him. We call Him good, but we use the word as if we knew what goodness really is. We call Him all-powerful, when we haven't a clue as to what His power is. We call Him eternal, without being able to imagine a state of being in which time does not exist. We can't shake hands with this Person and say "Hi," because we cannot imagine perfection in a living Being. We know it is not found on our level.

Something about this Person is painful to us. His perfection is a judgment on us, if only as the perfection of a diamond is a judgment on a pebble. So we get the impression that God is alien to us. We are not on speaking terms with Him. It would, in fact, be more appropriate for us to bow our heads and be silent in the face of this Being than to carry on a conversation with Him. It is necessary that we either put Him first or turn around and pretend He doesn't exist. Either we worship or we reject. We cannot treat Him as our equal—He is *not* the "man upstairs."

If we choose to worship, to put him first, it is gradually borne in upon us that this Being also loves us. The things He does to and for us, in view of His perfection and of our response to Him, take on a different color. They are now seen, if only in retrospect, to be good for us. We begin to see that He is not an irrational tyrant, but is possessed of a love so vast that He bothers to mold and shape our very insignificant lives. We fall down, and He picks us up. We do shameful and silly things, and He consoles us. We ask for something, and He gives it to us, frequently in an abundance of which we had not dared to dream.

The development of human knowledge about God is reflected, indeed, dramatized, in the Bible, beginning with humanity's alienation from Him and building up through successive discoveries and insights to the New Testament and the Gospel. The story of Abraham, for instance, is the story of one initial insight into God's personhood. Abraham's descendants discovered that God would make agreements (testaments) with them, that He would deliver them from their condition. In the writings of the prophets, as tragedy after tragedy disciplines the Jews, the realization of God's righteousness and perfection grows. Not until the later prophets is there held out much hope that God might be loving.

And then, with the experience of the disciples of Jesus, it becomes clear that God is the sort of God who not only loves but forgives, one whose forgiveness creates a new kind of life. The appearance of the Spirit in the Church completes the Christian revelation of God. He reveals Himself as the Trinity.

There is a lot more that can be, and frequently is, said about God. We use words like omnipotent, all-knowing, just, holy, and so on. He is all this and more. Yet we find it difficult to comprehend what these words mean, because in every case we are trying to capture in words a Being who is unlimited. Consider the creation, for instance. We talk about God as the "creator of heaven and earth" and immediately entrap ourselves in futile (if frequently overheated) arguments about the way in which creation did, and still does, come about. Are the creation accounts in the Book of Genesis to be taken literally? Or are we to assume that God constantly creates through the process called "evolution"? Christians hold to either view. The point to be noted within the debates is that we know very little about the ways in which God works, that our insights are like flashes of light, rather than like blueprints of God's design. Or consider God's power. We say, "God is all-powerful. Well, then, why doesn't He *do* something about this situation?" We assume He is doing nothing because we have linked our view of power to our own perceptions. If we had God's power, we would use it differently. Precisely because we would do so, we find Him incomprehensible.

As human experience limits us, so the limits of human imagination restrict us in our knowledge of God. We know all the words, but we can't figure out what they mean in practice. What do the words *pure spirit* conjure up? A wisp of smoke? The wind? We feel we have made some progress in understanding when we reach the point where we can say that *spirit* means "not visible or touchable." But we cannot get beyond this negative description to a positive one, because nothing in our imagination allows us to visualize a Being unlimited by our dimensions of time and space.

Nor are we always helped by theology. Theological arguments suffer from the same obstacles as do doctrinal statements about God. Both are probably best left to those who enjoy this sort of thing. We all know what happens when we try to argue with agnostics. We only seem to confirm them in their attitudes. Arguments about God's nature are similarly hindered. The argument for the Trinity is a case in point. "If God were not a Trinity, He could not be a loving God. Love must have an object. If God could not love within Himself—as in the Persons of the Trinity—He would have to depend on something outside Himself in order to love. This would mean that He wasn't complete and perfect within Himself, but dependent on His creation."

This is a fine piece of reasoning, but it will not convert anyone. What does make a difference is the experience of God as Creator/Father, as Savior, and as inner Power. Until we have been able to identify the experience of God that we have known in our own lives, the words remain only words, and the doctrine of the Trinity remains a puzzle for experts.

Given the narrowness of human vision, it is no wonder that the "problem of evil" seems to us insoluble. Part of the problem is merely an academic question. It is unproductive to debate God's "responsibility" for the disasters that keep on interrupting human life. We can argue the matter until we have exhausted it and ourselves and still remain unsatisfied, simply because we are not able to probe God's purposes to discover any answer.

To be sure, human sin causes much of human tragedy: a lethal fire can be caused by an arsonist; a terrible flood can be traced to the greed of men who deforested the mountains a thousand miles away; the hideous devastation of war stems directly from human determination to shape the world according to human specifications; and a tragic highway accident is certainly not God's fault. Beyond this we can only speculate, and we do so with only a modicum of information about God. We have no way of reading His mind (if "mind" applies to God), for example, when cancer strikes a child.

Even so, what affects us directly is not the cause of evil, but the way in which we are going to live with it. If a person close to us dies, the ache in our hearts is not "Who caused this? God? The doctors? Who?"—although we may ask such questions out loud. The real question is "How can I go on living now?"

If we had all the answers to the "why" questions, all laid out for us in language we could understand, it would not help us with our real question. The problem of evil is not solved when it is explained. It is solved when we are enabled to live with it.

There are at least three ways in which the problem of evil can be dealt with. First, we can ignore it. We can say that there is no pain and suffering, that this is all an illusion, which will pass away. This, of course, has its perils. Denying the existence of anything is not an answer at all, but an evasion. Like all evasions, this one can lead into worse complications. We are having to force ourselves into an unnatural state of ignorance by denying what our bodies and emotions are crying out about.

Secondly, we can endure the pain and suffering stoically. This is the "stiff upper lip," "keep your chin up" brand of pain-relief. It has certain merits, of course, in that stoicism keeps us from deteriorating into the depths of self-pity. But it requires will power and self-control, and these are in short supply when the pain and suffering get really bad. Furthermore, stoicism provides little help when someone else is doing the suffering, and we are forced to stand silently by, helpless to help.

The third attitude is Christian, handed directly to us by Jesus of Nazareth, who neither denied the existence of pain nor endured it with a stiff upper lip. He made use of it. That is, he took it up as deliberately as if it were a package to be carried or a job to be done. He told his disciples, "Take up your cross and follow me." Or, in other words, "Don't just ignore or endure what is happening to you. Live in it without being overcome by it. Your suffering is one of your jobs within God's Kingdom. Pick it up and carry it." This is God's answer to our real question.

This Christian attitude appears, on the surface of it, to be cruel, even impossible, because it would be kinder, surely, to remove the pain and suffering altogether. But we might look again at what Jesus did with his cross. The pain and suffering were not the end of a story, but the beginning of a new life. What we are asking for, when we want to live without pain, is a return to Eden. What we are offered is something far greater. Of course, we cannot expect something as dramatic as the Resurrection to issue from our personal crucifixions. But the Resurrection itself promises that out of evil can come a good that is immeasurably greater than the pain.

Naturally, we cannot be expected to make use of our old enemy, pain, on the strength of our own capabilities. This would be equivalent to asking the lion and the lamb to lie down together, for we live in constant dread of pain. But the Gospel enlightens us even here. God can be discovered at work in evil as well as in good, in the crucifixion even of the innocent. Pain can cease to be an enemy, the stuff out of which our personal victories are made. The lion and the lamb can, after all, lie down together.

It begins to seem as if our knowledge of God is at the same time more extensive and more limited than first appeared. On the one hand, when we reflect seriously on our own lives, we find we have met God in more ways than we had noticed. On the other hand, our facile use of second-hand descriptions and arguments is no guarantee that we know what we're talking about. Indeed, the more assertive we are, the greater the danger that we speak with someone else's words.

As long as our knowledge is restricted to that which we pick up second-hand, it will tend to insulate us from reality. We think that once we learn to assent to the proposition that God is love, we will be able to be happy. In point of fact, we are not.

God's love is in a different category from our human versions. It is not just bigger or wider or purer. Until we grasp the difference, we find ourselves saying "God wouldn't do this to me," even after He has done it. If we accept at face value the information that God is spirit, we assume that He is not interested in material things. We will then be unable to make sense out of the promise of the Kingdom of Heaven on earth, because we will have made ourselves blind to His judgment and forgiveness here and now.

Yet once we learn the Christian art of identifying who our Lord and Savior really is, and once we commit ourselves to Him, then our knowledge of God deepens into first-hand experience. We discover Him for ourselves. Our understanding of His will is sharpened, and we learn to perceive Him even in the most unlikely circumstances. The everyday job of living takes on significance, however trivial it may have been, because we know who we are, where the power to live comes from, and who is Lord. And now we can begin to understand Him.

EIGHT

The Last Things

Apart from wanting to find a religious solution to the problem of evil, people also seem to want a solution to the problem of death, our common and unavoidable destiny. At least, we usually demand that organized religions provide us with some guarantee of a future state that will be different from the one we're in, whether that state be rest, release, or simply a happier version of life as we now know it. At the same time, of course, we cling with considerable determination to this life that we're in. Death may be our universal fate, but nonetheless we fear it, because when the body dies, we can no longer be who we have been; a part of us will decay. So, part of our wish for assurance about a life-after-death, in whatever form we envision it, is our reluctance to let go of life-now.

The Christian promise of God's Kingdom is not, of course, based primarily on assurances about life-after-death. Rather, it is based on the possibility of a new life here and now. The Kingdom of God is found within our everyday lives as we increasingly turn them over to Christ. The Christian call, then, answers most of our deepest inner longings quite explicitly and directly, in the life and teachings of Jesus, in his death and

Resurrection, and in the ongoing work of his Church. But we still have to face the end of the story—the end of our personal life stories. We still live with the compulsion to go on living, and Christians die, the same as everyone else.

The consciousness of the threat posed by death is always with us, although we are frequently unaware of it. Almost as a matter of course, we indulge in countless things that are designed either to provide for death or to postpone it. Insurance, diets, safety regulations, vitamins, annual checkups—all the "life preservers" on which we rely—are evidence of our own preoccupation with death. We admit it is inevitable. We merely try to manage it, as if it were dust under the furniture or an untidy corner. There still remains something fundamentally irrational about it. We struggle all our lives long to find some rhyme or reason in human life, and then we die. We battle to grow up, we fall in love, we earn a living, we raise a family, we make our dreams come true (or, more probably, we keep on hoping that those dreams will materialize); yet, it all ends, as if none of it mattered at all.

The irrationality of death is one disturbing factor that each of us must come to grips with. But even worse, perhaps, is the fact that death is the unknown. We must all come to it, yet no one can tell us what it is like. No wonder we are afraid of it. No wonder that we must learn how to die, how to get through the denials, the anger, the bargaining, and the helplessness so well documented by researchers in the field. It could not be otherwise, save for those who have never thought about death. It is a very terminal event—for all we know, the end of our journey.

The questions we find ourselves asking, as we do face the reality of death, reflect not only a very human curiosity about the unknown, but a ragbag of opinions and ideas about Christian teaching in regard to death—another collection of bits and pieces of unthought-out, second-hand information. And the questions themselves point to our hidden assumptions about what are called the Last Things.

If death is the cessation of life, then it must be the beginning of whatever comes after life. So it would seem that the sequence runs something like this: we live here on earth, then we die, and then we enter whatever state it is that concludes our personal stories. If we believe in a heaven, it would seem to represent our own personal version of a happy ending. (We might recall that Huckleberry Finn was not at all attracted to the idea of sitting around playing a harp.) Whatever we look forward to, at least we hope for a release from the burdens of this world and an entrance into an existence free from the problems we now have.

Conversely, hell is seen as the unhappy ending, the kind of ending we can never really believe is ahead for us. So strong is our craving for a happy ending, and so rebellious do we feel at the premise that it might not work out well for us, that many people deny the whole idea of hell. If we seriously examine our own conduct, we are led to call up everything we remember about God's mercy. Surely He won't deny us the happy ending? Surely whatever we have done, we don't deserve hell?

Whichever way it goes, the determination of our individual endings is what we call judgment. Assuming that we have lived a good life, have been kind more than we have been cruel, and have not broken the Ten Commandments too frequently, God must certainly look upon us and say, "This one is all right." And if we have little of virtue to recommend us, we all know that God forgives even the worst of us (although we have to swallow hard at the proposition that He might conceivably forgive monsters like Hitler and Stalin). God will presumably understand that we didn't mean to or didn't know better, much as a parent might overlook a childish misdemeanor. Still, we are from time to time concerned about it all. Beneath our confidence in God's mercy is the occasional, unpleasant suspicion that judgment may be painful, that even His forgiveness may extend into areas we prefer to keep hidden.

Since death is what brings about the ending of our present lives, it has power over us beyond any other human event. It introduces us to whatever eternal condition we have won for ourselves, and much of its terror issues from the fear that we may not have won much of anything. If, on the other hand, we refuse to entertain the idea of any form of life-after-death, we still have the *fact* of death to contend with. Many people take their comfort from the thought that we can hope to live in the memories of our families and friends, long after we have gone. Others speak of "immortality in the lives of our children." Rationalizing that we "live on" in the personalities of other people, we think we have reconciled the finality of death with our urge to live.

In any event, whenever we try to make sense out of the Christian Church's teachings about the Last Things, we have to cope with a great deal of undocumented guesswork. Most of us seem to wind up in one of two states of mind. Either we get ourselves hopelessly involved in speculation, flights of fancy, and superstition, or we reject the whole thing. Our human habits of fear and rebellion color much of what we say, and we have trouble hearing, let alone assimilating, what the Gospel has to say.

As long as the story's ending is regarded as the point of the story, we will find ourselves unable to understand it. As long as the journey's end is the only reason for the journey, we will never know why we are really traveling.

We all find it very difficult indeed not to look for the meaning of our lives in some future or other, rather than in the here and now, and some of the effects of this habit show up in our wary opinions. We will, for instance, have difficulty in agreeing as to the nature of a "happy" ending. The teachings of the Church do not necessarily help us here, because traditionally the essence of heaven has been taught to be life with God and with those who have gone before us. But do we really want to spend eternity in God's company? Do we really want to spend eternity with our "loved ones"? (This depends in large part on how we have gotten on with them here.) And how about those people we know to be good Christian souls, whom we find boring or irritating? Eternity with them? We have equally troublesome problems when we start talking about what we want heaven to be like. Is it to be a place of rest? Or would eternal rest violate our love of activity and action? It is just as difficult to reconcile our many speculations about the unhappy ending.

For some of us, hell would be eternal close proximity to people. For others, it would be eternal isolation.

Whenever we find ourselves looking for meaning—the meaning of our lives here and now—in terms of life-after-death, we discover how little sense we really make of it all. This is why we ask all the questions we do. If our future state is the reason for living today, then we have to find out all we can about that future state. And if we don't like what we hear, we refuse to accept it. How can we accept the notion that the point of our lives, the meaning of our existence, is as likely to be hell as heaven, let alone the notion that heaven, as so frequently presented to us, might include some features we would find unattractive?

In the Gospel according to John is the story of Lazarus, brother of Mary and Martha, those sisters who represented differing views of discipleship. As John tells the story, Lazarus had fallen ill but although the sisters sent him word, Jesus did not hurry to his side to heal him. On the contrary, he apparently waited until it was clear that Lazarus had died. Then he set out for the village of Bethany, his disciples with him. When he arrived, he found that his friend had been buried four days before. Mary and Martha greeted him not only sorrowfully but reproachfully: if Jesus had only been there, Lazarus would not have died. (All those who followed Jesus were aware of his ability to heal.) Jesus answered: "Your brother will rise again . . . . I am the resurrection and the life; he who believes in me, though he die, yet shall he live, and whoever lives and believes in me shall never die. . . ." (John 11:23–26) Led by the mourners to the cave-tomb in which Lazarus had been buried, Jesus asked that the stone sealing the tomb be rolled away. Since Lazarus had been dead for four days, it was pointed out to him that the body would have begun to decay, would "stink." But Jesus commanded that the stone be removed. So they took away the stone. Jesus prayed aloud to the Father and called out, with a loud voice, "Lazarus, come out." "The dead man came out, his hands and feet bound with bandages, and his face wrapped with a cloth. Jesus said to them, 'Unbind him, and let him go.'" (John 11:1–44)

The story of Lazarus' return from the dead has a message that seems specifically tailored for the human fear of death. If we read it in its entirety, we cannot avoid its implications. Indeed, it seems as if Jesus' deliberate delay in arriving at the scene were almost planned, as if he were preparing to shake, even destroy, our prejudices about death.

When we read the story of Lazarus, one rather nitty-gritty question comes immediately to mind: could the man Lazarus, after his raising, ever look upon death as we do? Even today we hear testimonials from men and women who have undergone clinical death and who have been "brought back." These people do not perceive death as the rest of us do. It is supposed that Lazarus died—finally—later. But death would have been familiar to him, as it presumably would be for anyone who had been pronounced dead and had "come back." Whatever the unknown is, Lazarus knew about it.

Those of us who have never gone through the Lazarus experience may or may not be the losers in this human debate about death. On the other hand, we really do not know (never having gone through physical death) what it feels like. But, if we look closely at the Last Things, it is clear that we, like Lazarus and the others, know a lot more about death, judgment, heaven, and hell than we quite realize. The story of Lazarus is a sign, a guidepost, to Christians. We know all too well what the Last Things are all about, because we meet them daily. We do not daily die physically, or hear St. Peter rattle his keys, or burn, or strum harps. But we do live through death, judgment, hell, and heaven, all our lives long.

There are more ways to die than with the body, as we all know. We show our knowledge in conversation: "It's killing me!" "I might as well be dead." "Better dead than Red!" Admittedly, much of what we say about death is exaggerated, and most of us who talk glibly about the merits of death talk out of ignorance or anger. But behind all the rhetoric lies the awareness that we perceive death as something more than physical cessations of brain waves or heartbeats. We die small deaths all the time. Each time we give up a fond desire, we die a little. The man or woman who cannot find work, no matter how hard he or she tries, dies little deaths every day in the unemployment statistics. It may only be the death of hope, perhaps, but death occurs in many forms. The teenager whose boyfriend ditches her for someone else dies inside. Perhaps it is only her self-confidence or self-esteem, but she too dies a little. Anyone who hears a doctor's verdict about a heart, a lump, a blood test, or an X-ray—when the verdict entails a permanent alteration in one's life—dies to whatever life style must be put away.

We can all multiply these examples out of our own experience. Each of us knows what it means to die in these individual, private ways. At each moment in which there is an end to a real part of our own lives, there we go through a form of death. Sometimes the death could be called murder: someone killed something in us. Sometimes the death was accidental: a tiny circumstance may have cut us off from a part of life. Sometimes the death may result from natural decay: our abilities die a bit as we grow older. Or we may invite death by deliberate withdrawal from life, by courting it via alcohol or drugs or suicide.

Lazarus represents us all. We all know what death is like. We have gone through many of its forms, simply by living.

The experience of judgment, too, is a familiar one. All human beings know what judgment feels like, because we all go through it. Children are raised within the formulas of adult judgment. Adults live with judgment as part of their normal, everyday existence. An employer, a nominating committee, the friends making up their Christmas card list, the baby-sitter, the owner of the house across the street—these are the people who judge us. Sometimes their verdict is favorable. Sometimes it is not. Whatever the outcome, our judges have one thing in common. They always are people who have some sort of power over us. They matter to us, either in and of themselves, as in the case of families and friends, or they represent some value we hold dear, whether the value is real or illusory. What they say about us affects the way we are looked at by others, and what they say to us affects the way we feel about ourselves.

The most potentially damaging verdicts are those passed down by the people we esteem most highly. The baby-sitter's opinions about the way we raise our children are, perhaps, not terribly important. Most of us can live with being taken off a Christmas card list. But what an employer thinks has more substance. And the most important judgments are those made by the people we love. They are the judges who can condemn us most thoroughly. Only those who really count in our lives are able to make our hearts break.

When we look at what we experience of judgment in life, it all seems to depend on the way we keep the rules, whether the rules of a loving relationship or the customs of the world we live in. If we cannot or do not follow the rules, we run the risk of condemnation. We don't get promoted, we don't get praised, we are not spoken to or recognized, we don't get loved. In fact, we are thrown back on ourselves, isolated, hurt, forced to face our failures without any help from outside. We know very well what it feels like to be judged.

When we go through what we have come to know as death-in-life, we find ourselves in one of two conditions. Either the little death we underwent was the beginning of a new kind of life, or it was the beginning of meaningless frustration and pain. For instance, sometimes people have to die a little (or a lot) in giving up their more damaging vices. Yet they find that they are actually only beginning to live, as when a heavy smoker gives up cigarettes and can, for the first time in years, appreciate food and fresh air. On the other hand, if we have had to bid a permanent farewell to someone we love, the years ahead could be totally devoid of purpose and joy—if we allow them to be.

Whatever our personal examples of heaven-in-life and hell-in-life may be, it is clear that heaven involves the fruition and development of our abilities. It involves the knowledge that those who matter to us find us worthwhile. It includes the fulfillment of our expectations, both for ourselves and for others. It sustains a delicate balance between individuality and relationship. It is, above all, a new lease on life.

Hell, on the other hand, involves the inability to be what we can be. We cannot keep to the rules; we cannot win the acceptance and approval of those who matter to us. Nor can we forget the mistakes and sins we have committed, because there is no way for us to straighten them out or justify them. Our lives seem not to expand, but to shrink in around us. We fly from relationships that bring us nothing but painful judgments, and we draw back into suicidal selfishness. Or, perhaps even worse, we refuse to be individuals and submerge our personalities in sick and self-destructive relationships.

If the story of Lazarus has a message for us, it is that we can share with him the change of heart about death. As he could look on death from a new perspective, having been through it, so can we, once we learn to go through it in our own lives. Indeed, the Christian teachings about the Last Things are not outrageously difficult after all. They merely reflect what we already know.

What does all this say to our questions? We have two principal areas of concern: our fear of the story's ending and our wish for a new life. Once we have learned to identify death-in-life, physical death is a shade less mysterious. And if we have reached the point at which we can identify heaven-in-life, the Kingdom of Heaven becomes something more than a vague promise. It becomes a real possibility. Yet death-in-life is a terrible experience, just as judgment-in-life is frequently agonizing. And hell-in-life is an experience that can make us long for the release of physical death. Heaven, as we experience it under ordinary circumstances, never lasts long enough for us to feel safe. We have little to hope for, if the Last Things of God are merely a reproduction on the grand scale of the "last things" we go through here and now. We have broken the rules of God with appalling regularity. We have to face God's very inscrutable judgment. We have to cope with the very real possibility of an eternal hell (which, if our own experience is any example, would be pain without measure).

All the speculations, all the guesswork, all the intellectual understanding we develop about death, judgment, heaven and hell, are worth exactly nothing without the promise of Christ. "I am the resurrection and the life; he who believes in me, though he die, yet shall he live. . . ." (John 11:25) It is worth noting that Jesus said "believes in me," not "believes me." The basis for participation in this new life is not intellectual assent, but trust. Furthermore, as Jesus goes on to call Lazarus back to life, he does so as if to confirm his own promise by putting it into action. In his own Resurrection, the promise is ratified and made eternal, so that, just as Lazarus' death was converted into life, our own little deaths may be transformed.

The Resurrection is the concrete example of God's assurance that out of death can come life—a new life. This is a difficult concept for us to grasp. We are accustomed to thinking of death as painful, terrifying, evil, or destructive. We would like to think of the Resurrection as the removal of death, as a sort of cosmic denial of the fate we all must endure. But the Resurrection was not a denial of death. It was painful, terrifying, evil, and destructive when Jesus of Nazareth died on the Cross. The point of Resurrection is that death was itself transformed. Out of death came new life.

Lazarus' experience could help us here. Out of his death came his raising from the dead. The one had to happen first, or the other could not. (Similarly, unless there had been that "Good" Friday, there could have not been that Easter.) Death, then, is a necessary part of our new life. Without dying all our little deaths, we cannot live the new life, we cannot maintain ourselves within the Kingdom of Heaven here and now. And it is trust in Christ that makes all this possible, since it is He who brings about the little resurrections we can perceive in our daily lives. It is He who brings us through our final death, into whatever new life may follow.

Christians who have faced death-in-life squarely, who have learned to relate it to the death of God's Son, can open their hearts and minds to the idea of physical death, knowing that without the moment of death, there can be no new life. As they commit themselves to Christ, they can allow physical death to happen, neither fighting it, nor seeking it, nor avoiding it. This is only the final example of all the deaths they have undergone in life. It is not something new to be feared. It may be painful—

almost all our little deaths are, no matter how ordinary they may seem—and it may be terrifying. There may be plenty of evil surrounding its circumstances. Yet Christians who have become accustomed to living by the power of the Holy Spirit can die with the same power. They can close their eyes with the sure and certain knowledge that death is the necessary stuff out of which resurrection comes. St. Paul wrote, "Though our outer nature is wasting away, our inner nature is being renewed every day. For this slight momentary affliction is preparing for us an eternal weight of glory beyond all comparison, because we look not to the things that are seen, but to the things that are unseen. . . ." (2 Corinthians 4:16–18)

Similarly, Christians who have made a loving God their principal judge in life have not much left to fear of God's judgment after death. Their faith—that is, their commitment to Christ and the Christian way—are all the testimony necessary to acquit them. They know very well what their vices are. They certainly know what they have done and left undone. Yet they know that it is not their virtues or accomplishments or good deeds that will win approval from God. It is the worth of Jesus of Nazareth, to whom they have allied themselves, that saves them from an adverse judgment. And because they know something of the love of God, they also know that He is the only judge that ever mattered. St. Paul, again: "If God is for us, who is against us? He who did not spare his own Son but gave him up for us all, will he not also give us all things with him? . . . It is God who justifies; who is to condemn?" (Romans 8:31–34)

No one, not even the most astute of Christians, can know with certainty what kind of heaven is to be expected as death approaches. We do know what we would like, Christian or not. We may or may not want reunion with loved ones; we may or may not want to meet the object of our faith. If we are to "hear" music, we might prefer Bach to hard rock—or vice versa. But for a committed Christian there is the certainty that whatever kind of ending they will have, it will be right, because the rightness of that ending does not depend on their limited, perverse, and ignorant imaginations.

And hell? We have been provided with plenty of possible images: devils, fires, brimstone, ice, and torment have all figured in the human effort to describe an ultimate hell. The images are usually drawn from whatever elements represent the opposite of what we think is beneficial or productive of peace and happiness, hence the emphasis on extremes of pain. Unfortunately, we can find ourselves trapped by the images (particularly if they seem to require *bodily* suffering) so that we reject the whole idea of hell. Is there really an eternal hell? Presumably there well may be. But this is not the issue. If we needed convincing, life as we experience it is proof enough of hell. It is hell-in-life that points up our need for the Savior, not our fear of an unhappy ending to our life story. Again, if there *is* a hell, that too will be right for us, because God is eternally right.

The questions we like to tinker with when we are thinking about the Last Things turn out to have little value, because they grow out of speculation and can only be answered speculatively. Such matters as unbaptized babies, second chances, purgatory, St. Peter and the pearly gates, and so on, can never be finally settled by us. Indeed, whenever we get bogged down in the mechanics of the story's end, we can be sure we have lost sight of the source of life's meaning.

We find the answers to our own questions as we move through our own journeys. Death is, after all is said and done, a part of that journey. We face physical death and the other Last Things with the same expectations we bring to other steps in life. Consequently, we know that as Christ rose from the dead, so He will raise us. We have no idea how, when, or even why this resurrection will happen to us. But we know that it will, because we have already recognized resurrection within our individual histories.

NINE

Christian Personality

What happens to us, as individuals, as we discover ourselves during our journey, as we respond to Christ, as we allow ourselves to be re-directed? Whether it be because we are fond of happy endings or because we wish to know what we can expect of ourselves, sooner or later we come to the question of what difference the Christian gospel makes in the human personality. With the wealth of power made available to us as Christians, it would seem reasonable to expect some change in our individual lives—a change of attitude, perhaps, changes in behavior, maybe, at least more peace of mind. If there is no difference in us, as human beings, the journey will seem to have been a waste of time and energy, an expensive trip to nowhere. What, then, can we expect a Christian personality to be like?

Are Christians, for instance, "better" than other people? Not necessarily. Becoming Christian does not automatically make saints out of plumbers, professors, or politicians. Nor does becoming Christian automatically make them better at their jobs, although they may find themselves more cheerful or more considerate or more content. Are Christian saints what we have sometimes pictured them, particularly when we think about the Puritans—pious, earnest, humorless, other-worldly? The most superficial acquaintance with Christian saints indicates otherwise. Saints are ordinary people. Some of them were—and are—witty, sophisticated, worldly folk. Others were—and are—not especially bright, not especially distinguished, not especially talented. Saints come in all sizes and shapes. Are Christians supposed to be interested only in church-y things, to draw back from the evils of this world? Judging from the degree to which Jesus—and the Church, following him—concerned himself with the world, it would seem that Christians are very interested indeed in what goes on around them.

Are Christians reformers, out to make the world over, whether the world wants to be made over or not? Sometimes—given the excesses of missionary zeal that Christians have committed—it would seem so. Some Christians do run to extremes. Most do not. We carry our personalities with us, like snails their shells, even as we respond to Christ, and most Christians are not zealots. Indeed, the better we know ourselves as part of the Kingdom of God, the less likely we are to assume that we are in possession of all God's truth or to take unto ourselves God's power of judgment. Christians cannot be stereotyped. They come in a variety of backgrounds; they may be rich or poor; they subscribe to all sorts of political beliefs; they belong to all sorts of nationalities; they are not limited as to sects or branches of the Church.

Still, given all the possible variations, we have to make the effort to find out what distinguishes the "redeemed" from other people, if only to discover what Christ does in and for us as individual travellers.

The discovery of Christ in the midst of our personal lives can be (and sometimes is) a dramatic breakthrough, a sudden release from the vicious cycle of pain and despair that characterizes so much of human existence. In that case, our responses to him will probably be correspondingly dramatic, and we will start talking about the "born again" experience. With others, the discovery is gradual, like the sun's rising rather than like a bolt of lightning. In this case our responses are gradual and measured. Although here too we are being "reborn," we are less likely to talk about the experience, because we sense it is a process rather than an event. In either case, however, the initial response is called *faith*.

There are a lot of things faith is not. It is not a substitute for intelligence, as when we contrast it with "reason." Any response to Christ that omits the human capacity to think, to question, to explore, would be less than complete. Nor is faith a retreat from painful reality, as when we talk about the "life of faith" as opposed to "real life." A response to Christ that did not include reality would wind up denying the ugly truth of his crucifixion. Faith is not a quality won by hard work, as when we say "You just have to have faith." It is not a quality at all, but a response. It is not belief, so we cannot "lose our faith." If it gets lost, it wasn't faith at all, but merely the intellectual acceptance of a set of propositions.

Faith is simply the commitment of ourselves to God in Christ and to the way of life associated with him. It is a simpler commitment for some than for others, because it develops out of our awareness of the depth to which we have sunk without God. Furthermore, if we have nowhere else to turn but God, the process of commitment is welcome, a big relief from a terrible struggle. If we have alternatives that are still attractive—a set of little gods that still seem to offer us some life and some hope—faith can include a wrenching withdrawal from our own desires. So the external symptoms of the faith response depend almost entirely on our individual circumstances, and there can be no absolute standards by which to measure them. But all faith-responses share some things in common.

Fundamentally, we respond first by making a decision to turn our lives over to the God who admittedly is a stranger to us. In order to do this, of course, we have to admit that we are incapable of saving ourselves. This admission goes far beyond the customary acknowledgment that God exists or that God has personhood. It is one thing to say, in general, that humanity is incapable of managing by itself. It is much more difficult to say, "I am alone and afraid and unable to run my own life."

At the same time that we make the first tentative response to God, our illusions about ourselves will have to be stripped away. This is why God's power is necessary even for us to commit our lives to Him. And this is why faith is often referred to as a gift from God.

The second part of our response is the undertaking of the Christian way of life. We adopt into our own daily lives the customs and ethics that are the heritage of the Christian community. We do not delude ourselves into assuming that these customs and ethics *are* Christianity or that they can substitute for Christ himself. Rather, we deliberately place our lives into a context that has developed out of a historical, communal experience. We are linking our individual faith responses to those of other Christians, thereby reinforcing both the commitment and ourselves. Perhaps we make a radical turn-around in our way of life; more likely we do not. We probably begin only gradually to allow that way of life to be transformed. In any event, whether hesitantly or boldly, we follow Christ as best we can, we worship God every Sunday (in commemoration of the Resurrection), and we work, pray, and give for the spread of the Kingdom. We ought not, of course, to expect the miraculous rebirth of our personalities. We are only disciples. We are placing ourselves under the "discipline" of God's people, on the assumption that the Church, as the body of Christ, has something to say to and do for us.

So faith is both a simpler and a broader thing than intellectual assent or wishful thinking. It covers a lot of territory, in that any serious commitment touches all aspects of life. Also, it is less difficult than it has been thought to be—assuming, of course, that we really do want to respond to Christ. Faith is the opposite of sin.

Out of the decision called faith springs the beginning of an inner condition that is known by a number of different names. It is perhaps best described as "assurance" or "confident expectation." Since we are no longer fighting against the world in which we live or against ourselves and each other, it is no longer necessary that we run for cover every time we make a choice that turns out to be wrong. Nor need we be paralyzed in the face of pain or fear or failure. To be sure, there is just as much as ever going on around us and inside us. There are the same things to be decided about, the same tragedies to be faced, the same people to encounter, and the same physical and financial burdens to be carried. But if the world and other people are the same, we are not, if only because our viewpoint has changed. We are now able to stay on an even keel in the midst of the same old problems. Some undefined, perhaps undefinable, core within remains calm and stable no matter what is going on in our minds and emotions. The difference between this assurance or expectation and the cheap imitations presented as "positive thinking" or "looking on the bright side" is obvious. We do not stimulate or manufacture this condition. It happens to us, usually in such a subtle fashion that we are almost unaware that we have changed, until we look back at the way we were. When crises come along, we can see how much our inner condition differs from the pre-faith condition. Where we once would have collapsed or dithered or run away, now there is an internal sense of calm and peace.

This inner condition is called *hope*. We have been redeemed out of the hell of the human condition. It isn't that nothing more can happen to us, but we can now face what we must with the conviction that we too can experience the Kingdom of God, that out of death comes resurrection. Because we have been redirected, we can move with the confidence that, wherever we go, we are going in the right direction, as long as we are following Christ. Hope is not (it need hardly be said) a sort of cosmic wishful thinking. Nor is it self-inflicted blindness to any obstacle we might encounter. It is more closely linked with belief, if by belief we mean conviction or trust. Christians are people who have been somewhere, so to speak, who can glimpse something about the love of God, who have discovered that God is the foundation of being, as opposed to the shifting ground of human thought or human achievement. Once that discovery has been made and has issued into faith, then it becomes unnecessary to look for assurance where none is to be found. Hope is the antidote to despair, and it too is the gift of God.

Once we have responded in faith to Christ's invitation and have learned to live in hope and expectation, our relationships with God and with other people will inevitably be affected. We will begin to understand how to *love*.

We are not unfamiliar with the phenomenon of love. Indeed, we think we know pretty much what it is, even if only in an imperfect, disordered version, even if only in terms of our own needs. Indeed, we have always been capable of a certain amount or degree of love. Our troubles have derived from the fact that what we know of love has been flawed—insufficient, distorted, or destructive. Human love suffers from human nature, and just as the condition of sin impedes our ability to get along with ourselves, so it twists our capacity to love other people, to say nothing of our capacity to love God. Sometimes we are unable to love others because we find others unlovable. Sometimes it is the other way around, and nobody seems to be able to love us. Sometimes we simply cannot love others because we detest ourselves. And sometimes others are similarly afflicted in their relationships with us. Whatever the consequences, being disordered forces us to love in disordered forms.

The pervasiveness of the human distortion of love can perhaps best be clarified if we examine the ways in which we try to relate love to God. Jesus said, "You shall love the Lord your God with all your heart, and with all your soul, and with all your mind, and with all your strength. . . ." (Mark 12:30) A remarkable commandment, considering that the Ten Commandments make provision only for obedience, not for love. But the ways in which we try to love God reveal our natural bent. We do all sorts of things to try to win His favor, like children trying to attract the attention and love of their parents. We try to strike bargains with Him, we try to bribe Him with promises, we even resort to blackmail ("Okay, if You won't help me, I'll stop going to church"). Two human beings, trying to forge a loving relationship, might employ similar tactics on each other. So doing they would only demonstrate their inability to love in a mature fashion. And as for loving God in the manner Jesus described? Well, we aren't really up to it. It's hard enough to love the people we know.

So Christian love, like God Himself, is not simply a large-scale reproduction of the emotional attachments we have learned to call love. If it were, it would merely reproduce the general messiness of human relationships. Christian love, sometimes known as charity, cannot be accomplished without God's own power, without a radical transformation in us. St. Paul wrote the best analysis: "Love is patient and kind; love is not jealous or boastful; it is not arrogant or rude. Love does not insist on its own way; it is not irritable or resentful; it does not rejoice at wrong, but rejoices in the right. Love bears all things, believes all things, hopes all things, endures all things." (1 Corinthians 13:4–7) (It might be worth noting that we need only hold our human loves up to Paul's mirror to see how defective they are.) Christian love is not sentimental, because it requires that we see the world around us without illusion and without romantic distortion. Nor is it necessarily rooted in *liking*. It does not depend on the way we feel about people, but on the way God loves them. Again, it does not depend on circumstances, even though we may make use of circumstances like money or gifts or food to demonstrate it. Christian love concerns itself with the real (not necessarily the spoken) needs of others. It accepts people as they are, not as they ought to be.

Christian love includes a good deal more than anything we are accustomed to. It includes, for example, the mighty operation of Christian forgiveness. This is not something we do by ourselves. We are merely passing on to others what has already been given to us. God forgives us, so we are able to forgive others, even to the startling extremes proposed by Jesus in his remarks about turning the other cheek. Love enables us to get beyond the common sense responses of self-righteousness or self-protection, even beyond hurt and self-pity, because we have no real need for common sense. Once our concern for others has been transformed, we are free to be less anxious about ourselves than we are about the people who hurt us. In part we can forgive because we have had our eyes opened to the universality of the human condition. We can see what causes human beings to act as they do. But chiefly we ourselves have been so warmed by the love of God that it is simply not necessary to fret over our bruises.

Christian love and forgiveness are contagious. They can no more be appropriated to our own advantage than can the common cold. Once the love of God has been experienced and identified, it is quite literally impossible to avoid a change in feeling toward our neighbors, short of deliberate (and damning) refusal to accept the fact of change.

There are other results from the faith response that have to do more specifically with our personal characters. These are usually summarized briefly in the four "cardinal" virtues or strengths: temperance, courage, wisdom, and justice. These attributes are what we thought we needed when we first began to be dissatisfied with ourselves. We wanted to get some control over our appetites (temperance). We wanted to learn to live with our fears (courage), to get some order into our lives (wisdom), and to be able to determine what is the right thing to do (justice). Oddly enough, however, these virtues are always considered to be secondary gains, almost by-products. They have to do not with what goes on inside us, but with the ways in which we live. They are what shows in public.

So in the Christian personality these strengths, real as they are, turn out to be bonuses, because they are of less real importance than the towering strengths of faith, hope, and love. True, Christians may acquire considerable skill in controlling their physical appetites. They may also find it possible to do incredibly difficult things with courage—the history of the church is packed with examples, from martyrdom to quiet struggles with poverty and suffering. Certainly Christians are more and more capable of identifying and evaluating the areas of life that really matter, as opposed to those that are illusory, and they acquire increased perception of what is right and what is wrong. But these are subsidiary attributes. They develop from the primary decision of faith, the stability of hope, and the energy of love.

It would be wonderful indeed if the process described above could be compressed into one instantaneous experience. Then we could expect to be new persons tomorrow, as soon as we had time to fall to our knees and pray to God to take over our lives. But, as anyone who has done much journeying can testify, the matter is more complex than this. Christians may have been born again, but there is a lot of growing to be done. The development of Christian personality has much in common with the development already observed in the life of prayer. That is, it does not proceed in a straight, upward line, but in stages or cycles that recur throughout life.

The initial step of commitment or faith is only the beginning of the Christian way. With the best intentions in the world, we are no sooner involved in the life of the Gospel than we may find ourselves caught up again in the problem of our transgressions—or worse, in the old human inability to make sense out of our existence. This is a disheartening experience. Quite apart from the terrible discouragement that so frequently follows our first efforts at faith, there is a feeling of betrayal. We were promised something better than the same old way.

This problem is technically known as *apostasy*, and nobody wrestled with it more vigorously than did the early Christians. We usually don't fall away from God deliberately. Instead, it is as if the weight of our own habits (or the power of our love of them) pulls us away from our chosen course. The great virtues seem to dissipate. Christian love deteriorates into those distortions that create such havoc in our lives. Then that inner core of assurance cracks like a quake-shattered building structure. Finally we question our commitment—if not our commitment to God, then at least our commitment to the Christian way of life. We look out at the landscape and wonder if we have journeyed anywhere at all, or if we, like Alice through the looking glass, have been running hard just to stay in the same place. Are we right where we started from? If so, then we must wonder what on earth was the use of starting.

It needs to be said, first of all, that we are never back at the starting point. The dynamics of faith and the power of God have made us different people, even though we are afflicted with the same set of habits. Once God has been admitted to our lives and our consciousness, it is impossible to kick Him out. We can very easily refuse to acknowledge His presence, but He does not allow us to exclude Him and He is not turned aside by our failures. Once the hold of original sin is broken, it is broken. We are never irretrievably caught in the same trap again.

The principal subjective result of falling away from our commitment is that we find ourselves face to face again with the question of behavior. Once again we watch ourselves being lazy, being jealous and covetous, manipulating those around us, judging events in terms of our pride, and so on. There is one notable difference, however, between where we find ourselves after having fallen away and where we were at the start. Where we once thoroughly enjoyed our transgressions, or made virtues of them, or tried to justify them, now we have been changed just enough so that we can no longer live comfortably with them. Instead, they make us downright uneasy. Our behavior doesn't feel right, as if our old vices and habits were a suit of clothes long outgrown.

Over this discomfort stands the remembrance of God's power. Once that power has produced the sense of freedom associated with faith, nothing less than faith looks quite the same. We know perfectly well that apostasy gets us nowhere, that only God's power can retrieve us from this new mess, that we can repent again, can hear Jesus' invitation anew, can participate once more in the Kingdom. Should we recommit ourselves, the decision will be a little easier, if only because we have begun to trust God on the basis of past experience. But the second time around, and at each successive choice, we commit ourselves to Him with deeper understanding, and with much greater accuracy. The apostate, having fallen away and returned, is in the position of the Prodigal Son, who appreciates his welcome home to a degree unknown to someone who has never failed. Our lapses become occasions for joy.

So we take another step in faith. Hope and love come flooding back, and the world—and we ourselves—seem to be straight once more. We will probably lapse again into apostasy, but again we will be able to respond to God. And each response brings us closer and closer to a full awareness of ourselves, others, and God. Christian personality develops out of the process of choice, out of the decisions we make daily.

And one of the characteristics of this conversion of ourselves is that we feel obliged to help other people get out of *their* personal messes. We become witnesses to the saving power of God; we ourselves engage in the same activities as did the original disciples. This is why Christianity is known as a "missionary" religion—although the word has unfortunate connotations.

Actually, Christian mission is not much different from any other kind of mission. All of us testify to whatever good news we have heard. We let it be known that there is a good new restaurant, if food is our comfort and concern. We tell people about a new, cheap discount store, if money matters to us. We tell the world about a promotion, or making the team, or falling in love. If we've found help for a painful illness, we certainly don't keep quiet about it. So it is with Christians who have experienced the process of faith. More often than not, however, they testify unconsciously. Only in the way they live do they indicate the degree of significance they attach to what they have found. Sometimes, of course, they can be very vocal, and since the development of Christian personality is gradual, what they say may be highly colored by the old habits of aggressiveness or self-satisfaction. In this event, what they say may be more offensive than helpful. And what they do may be marked less by love than by pride. But the more the great virtues take over, the more Christians can afford to understand, to look on their world with genuine concern and forgiveness. They even get over the natural assumption that their individual experience of God must be duplicated exactly in every other person. God's Kingdom, after all, is not comprised of clones. Nor is it to be equated with a particular branch of the Christian Church.

Christians also worship God together. The earliest Christians needed to gather together not only for the kind of support and sustenance that only a group of people can give. They also gathered for common worship, because they all had gone through the experience of knowing Christ, and so it is today. The Christian worships God all the time, to be sure. Praying, for example, is an act of giving "worth-ship" to God. But common worship is something more. For one thing, it too is a way of bearing witness to the world. Even the cars in a church parking lot on Sunday say to passers-by that Christians are doing for the world what no one else can do. Even more important to us as individuals, perhaps, worship carries us through much of the distress and turmoil associated with the times we fall away. In this regard it works for us much as does the ritual of, say, a meeting of Weight Watchers or Alcoholics Anonymous, in which the group's traditions sustain the individual in his or her struggle. Even if we personally find it virtually impossible to worship at certain times, the ritual of worship carries us along. We hear the Bible, for instance, and are reminded of where we have been. We say the prayers and are recalled to our position as sinners. We sing the hymns and feel that we are not alone.

Christians do other things, of course. They not only help each other, but anyone in need. They are increasingly able to share the burden of misery and pain that others must carry. They can assist even those who look on Christians as fools or suckers, much as the Good Samaritan helped the Jew in Jesus' parable. They can forgive their enemies. Mission and worship cannot be limited to one day a week, because the entire human personality is affected by faith, seven days a week. And all of our encounters with people are touched by what has happened to us.

Of course, Christians, like all human beings, have to come to terms with the world, even when the world seems indifferent or hostile. There seem to be no hard and fast rules for coping with those occasions when Christian commitment comes into conflict with other, antagonistic faiths. In our pluralistic society, it is not normally necessary that Christians die for their discipleship. But they may undergo a certain amount of discomfort, especially when they are thought to be soft in the head, or silly, or out of touch with trendy things. (And it must be said that some Christians—those who would bind the Christian personality to specific moral codes or to national political positions—bring discomfort upon themselves.) How we manage such occasions depends largely upon our own individual talents and interests, which, having been more or less freed from internal conflict by the grace of God, begin to display God's love to the world. So it is, for instance, that some Christians can be highly vocal seekers for social justice, while others simply work quietly for peaceful families and neighborhoods; and so it is that Christians turn up both as crusaders and as conscientious objectors. The New Testament is full of advice on the subject of life in the world, particularly in the letters written by apostles. That advice is limited by first-century cultural attitudes, but much of it remains relevant to twentieth-century travelers.

In the final analysis, Christians are recognizable primarily by their capacity to love, their sense of assurance, and their commitment to Christ. Of the three marks, love is the most important. The growth of Christian personality may be afflicted by hesitation, by backsliding, or by excesses of zeal. But as the personality matures, so does the ability of the Christian to live patiently, even triumphantly, within the stresses of contemporary life. If we cannot (should not?) make the world over to suit our visions, we can dimly perceive the outlines of the Kingdom all around us. In that perception we are able to "lay aside every weight, and sin which clings so closely, and . . . run with perseverance the race that is set before us, looking to Jesus the pioneer and perfecter of our faith. . . ." (Hebrews 12:1–2)

Where does the journey end? It ends, oddly enough, where it began, with our selves, but with our changed selves.

Thomas Wolfe gave one of his novels the title *You Can't Go Home Again.* While the caution expressed in that title really applies to all adult human beings, who can never find their way back to innocence, it carries special significance to those who have journeyed in faith. But an adult Christian would be more likely to say "Who wants to go back?" because the promise of Christ is not that we shall be wafted back to some primitive state of inexperience. Christianity offers us the prospect of something called *Sion,* not the forever lost Garden of Eden.

For Eden, or Paradise, to have continued through eternity, it would have been necessary for us to remain as we presumably were created: uncomplicated, unquestioning, naturally united to God. We did not so remain, and there is no way to turn the clock back or to excise from our consciousness the awareness of who we are and what evil is. But no faithful Christian would seriously wish to be restored to Eden, because Sion—the fully visible, realized Kingdom of God—promises us much more. We can be fully human, while at the same time the children of God. Although we still are creatures, we can be part of a new creation.

When we set out on our individual journeys, very few of us were looking forward to the same destination. The journey in faith is, in this regard, something like a "magical Mystery Tour." The destination reveals itself only as we travel. And when we reach it, if we do in this life, we find it to be strangely familiar, as if it had always been where we are, but unrecognized by our clouded eyes. T. S. Eliot, in "Little Gidding," catches the journey as well as anyone:

> *We shall not cease from exploration*
> *And the end of all our exploring*
> *Will be to arrive where we started*
> *And know the place for the first time.*